THE GIRAFFE HAS A LONG NECK . . .

THE GIRAFFE HAS A LONG NECK . . .

by

Jacques Poirier

With a Foreword by
Jean Lescure

Translated by John Brownjohn

LEO COOPER
LONDON

THE GIRAFFE HAS A LONG NECK . . .
was originally published in France
by Editions Fanlac, Périgueux, France, in 1992

First published in Great Britain in 1995 by

LEO COOPER

190 Shaftesbury Avenue, London WC2H 8JL
an imprint of
Pen & Sword Books Ltd,
47 Church Street,
Barnsley, South Yorkshire S70 2AS

© Jacques Poirier, 1992, 1995

Translation © John Brownjohn, 1995

A CIP record for this book is available from the British Library

ISBN 0 85052 461 X

Typeset by Phoenix Typesetting, Ilkley, West Yorkshire
Printed in England by
Redwood Books Ltd, Trowbridge, Wilts.

Contents

Foreword

It was around five o'clock on the afternoon of 9 April, 1944, when Camus walked into Jean Paulhan's first-floor office at Éditions Gallimard, No. 5, rue Sébastien-Bottin. Of all places in Paris, that was where one was most likely to encounter, at any given moment, someone more or less closely involved with the Resistance. There were five or six people in the room. Camus came straight over, steered me to the window and asked in a low voice if I could safely put someone up for the night – one night only. That presented me with a problem.

'It seems the Gestapo are looking for me,' I told him. 'I haven't been living at home for two months. My wife gave birth in a hospital corridor three weeks ago. They wrapped her and the baby in a blanket, and she's looking after it in a cramped apartment belonging to some relatives – hospitable folk, but they aren't in the know.'

'I'd forgotten,' Camus said.

He went over to someone else he knew, and I saw the two of them put their heads together. The other man looked worried and doubtful. Camus gave a resigned shrug and left the room without a word to anyone.

I caught him up on the stairs. 'Is it important?' I asked.

'Pretty important. He's the fellow in charge of the air drops for Malraux's maquisards. An English major.'

'If he's English he must have been in the blitz, and if he's with the maquis he must be used to roughing it. All right,' I said finally, 'he can sleep on the floor.'

We left the building and walked down the street. On the corner of rue de l'Université two men were waiting in the gentle warmth of the early spring sunshine: André Malraux and a lanky type whose ruddy cheeks convinced me, foolishly enough, that he was an Englishman nurtured on roast beef. We didn't introduce ourselves by name. In those days it was as well to bear in mind that the Gestapo might sooner or later 'invite' one to talk. The less one knew, the better. My Englishman's French was impeccable. I was an anglophile – in fact my best friend was English and had wanted to fight for France, but countless British Army drill instructors had been driven to distraction by his hopeless inability to march in step and salute correctly. This unknown Englishman made me even more admiring of a country that could train men for assignments as difficult as his – and, coincidentally, teach them to speak French without an English accent.

I asked him if he knew Neuilly. He did. The Sablons Métro station? Certainly.

'Fine,' I said. 'Ten tonight. I'll be waiting on the platform. When you get there, all you have to do is follow me.'

I had things to do in town that day, so we went our separate ways. Just after ten a train pulled into Sablons station and my Englishman got out. He followed as I headed for the exit and set off on a brief tour of the deserted streets. No one was tailing us. I waited for him at the door of the apartment house.

'The people who are putting us up are relations of my wife. They think we're there because we don't have any heating at home for the baby. They're discreet. You can be a cousin of mine – from Bordeaux, right?'

The baby was asleep. We put the mattress on the floor for my wife. The Englishman and I shared the bedsprings. He took up as little room as he could, but he fell asleep at once and spread his long limbs. I was the one who wound up sleeping on the floor.

But not for long, because an air raid started just after midnight. It outdid anything we had ever seen on Bastille Day: a crepitating, coruscating display of anti-aircraft fire and bombs, flares and searchlights, and it went on for a long time. My Englishman didn't stir, though every window in the street was thronged with spectators. It was dawn before the rest of us got to sleep.

On waking we learned that the raid, one of the 'area bombings' inaugurated by US Super-Fortresses, had well nigh flattened the marshalling yards at Villeneuve-Saint-Georges. No trains were running.

My Englishman, who had slept through it all, seemed worried that there weren't any trains but had a quiet lunch with us. We didn't talk much. 'All right if I come back this afternoon and pick up my things?' he asked. 'I think Malraux plans to come too.'

I said I would be there, and he left. He returned at around four, together with Malraux and two small tins of pâté de foie, which he presented to me. I don't know if anyone can now imagine what the close proximity of two tins of pâté de foie meant to someone whose belief in the continued existence of such delicacies was at that time restricted to gluttonous imaginings generated by daily pangs of hunger. I was half stupefied, half bemused. Simpering like a flustered housewife, I stammered, 'No, really, it's too much!' and sundry other banalities in the same vein. I must have looked a total idiot. Malraux seemed taken aback, but he recovered himself and said, in a tone that brooked no refusal, 'Captured from the enemy.'

I came down to earth, took the tins and put them on the table. Lying beside them was a small canvas by Bazaine, a present from me to my wife to mark the birth of our child. Malraux eyed it with the formidable intensity characteristic of his approach to painting. 'Bazaine,' he announced. I burst out laughing. 'That's obvious,' I said. At that period Bazaine used to sign his pictures in letters an inch high, but the style was unmistakeable too. Malraux overlooked my effrontery. He simply turned to me and asked if I could put the major up for another night. I said I could, and they left.

I have recalled this anecdote because Malraux's glimpse of the Bazaine had a sequel – one that clearly exemplified his rapport with the visual arts. He had looked at that picture for twenty or thirty seconds at most, and he never saw it again. Even when he came to dine at my home after the war, he never once entered the room where it hung.

Twenty years after that day in 1944 he was a government minister visiting a big Bazaine exhibition at the Museum of

Modern Art in Tokyo. For twenty years Malraux had often questioned me about my friends, the painters of the new Paris school. We toured the exhibition together – 'went round the assault course', as we termed it. On the way out he said, 'That little canvas of yours – those blues and pinks with the little fleck of green in the middle, the one that brings the whole composition to life – a pity you didn't lend it for the occasion. It's a good illustration of that particular turning-point in Bazaine's work.' Twenty or thirty seconds, and everything had crystallized in that prodigious visual memory of his. I, who saw the picture every day of my life, had to go and satisfy myself that the little green fleck was really there. It was.

The English major returned that evening. 'I've done something stupid,' he said when he came in.

I thought we were done for. 'You were followed?'

He laughed as if I'd said something idiotic. 'Of course not, I know the form. It was like this . . .' And he proceeded to tell me that, while passing the pet shop that used to be near the Arc de Triomphe end of the Champs-Élysées, he'd fallen in love with a dog in the window, gone in, and – to cut a long story short – bought it on the spot.

Being a dog-lover myself, I uttered exclamations of delight, but his misgivings persisted. 'The trouble is,' he said, 'it's this big.'

He made a gesture that conjured up visions of a beast the size of a small calf. It would clearly be hard to feed on the one hand, and, on the other, hard to conceal if one wished to remain inconspicuous.

We chatted a little that night, I to gloss over his 'stupidity', and he, I suppose, because he was fond of children. He played with our baby and was privileged to receive its first smile – an event that drew fatuous cries of wonderment from its parents.

We needn't worry, he assured us: the Allied landing was bound to take place this year. We were only too happy to believe him, but I still felt a trifle uneasy. 'He's so laid back,' I told myself. 'He doesn't realize who I am. He doesn't know the Gestapo are after me. If they catch up with me tonight, they'll nab him too. What a fool I was to take him in!'

I fell asleep for all that, and we passed an undisturbed night. He left the next morning, as nameless to me as I was to him, and that was that. I didn't see him again.

After the Liberation I was appointed literary director for radio by the Resistance – more precisely, by the *Comité National des Écrivains* [National Writers' Committee]. That made André Malraux my minister, so I saw him again. When I queried the identity of my temporary lodger he hesitated, then said a name that meant nothing to me and added that the man had become an ambassador somewhere overseas. We never reverted to the subject.

Thirty-four years went by, and an American academic named Herbert Lottmann came to Paris to write a book about Camus. Having run me to earth by dint of exhaustive inquiries, he confirmed that I had seen Camus on the date in question and had been asked to put someone up – in short, he told me what I already knew and have just recounted. He hadn't heard the story of the dog, which I duly contributed. (He embroidered it a little: according to him, the dog had also slept in our cramped little room.) The French edition of his book came out late in 1978.

Another three years went by, and I forgot all about the episode.

My receptionist – a new one, and not yet broken in – buzzed me one day and announced that 'a Monsieur Jacques Poirier' was on the line. 'Never heard of him,' I snapped. 'I told you always to ask exactly who's calling and why.' But it was too late – she'd already put him through. A voice said, 'I'm the person you put up thirty-seven years ago.'

I was engrossed in my work and light-years away from 1944. I'd put him up thirty-seven years ago? What was I, a hotel? The voice went on, 'I apologize for the intrusion. You let me hole up with you for a couple of nights, remember?'

His turn of phrase brought it all back: the uneasy nights, the excursions into town, the elaborate arrangements to meet. . . ., My English major had spoken perfect French, it was true. He said, 'My name is Jacques Poirier.' So he wasn't English at all.

He explained: he hadn't known who I was and had never thought to ask Malraux. After the war he had gone to live and work overseas. He was phoning me because he had just received a call from an American friend who had read Lottman's book on Camus and come across the story of the dog. 'I know the name of the man who put you up in 1944,' the friend had told him. 'It's Jean Lescure.' So Poirier had telephoned my publishers, Gallimard, and received the standard, well-trained response: 'Please write to this office, monsieur; we never divulge our authors' addresses.' He begged and pleaded, tried charm and friendly persuasion, but to no avail. 'You'll have to write,' the secretary insisted. It was the word 'Resistance' that finally overcame her own resistance. 'And that's how I obtained your address and phone number.'

Thirty-seven years is a long time. I was intrigued. We simply had to meet in person, and we did. My Englishman was less of a beanpole these days, nor was he English. We had questions to ask and stories to tell, but times had changed. We lowered our voices in the restaurant so as not to be taken for two silly old codgers, and also, perhaps, because we had slipped back into our former clandestine habits.

We saw a great deal of each other after that. One day I said to Jacques, 'You had a fascinating war. Why don't you write a book about it?' He was coy at first. 'I'm no writer, and anyway, who'd be interested at this distance in time?' It took me years to persuade him, but I finally succeeded. A good thing, too. Judge for yourself.

Jean Lescure

From that we may conclude
that we must wage
unremitting war on the wicked
Peace is very good in itself;
I agree, but what use is it
with treacherous enemies?

The Wolves and the Sheep
Jean de La Fontaine

INTRODUCTION

To tell the truth, I didn't write the following account for publication. I wrote it for my grandchildren, and for them alone.

Why? That's easy. I wanted them to read it partly for my own sake, partly to acquaint them with the period in question and keep its memory green, and partly to encourage them to reflect on the exploits of those members of their grandfathers' generation who, though few in number, displayed a spirit of adventure that entitles them to a certain affection.

Another thing: I'm tired of reading accounts of the period by mandarins of the Resistance who monopolize it, tearing each other apart in the process, or seize the opportunity to discredit the whole movement. I want my grandchildren to know that, whatever the merits of our mandarins, the Resistance was made up primarily of men like those I mention here: Raymond Maréchal, Charles the carpenter, Poulou the pâtissier, the Abbé Marchadoux of Sagelat, Émile Chateaurenaud, the Marquis de Commarque, and many others – in short, all those of whom no one ever speaks nowadays.

That, probably, is the reason why I have avoided falling into the trap of writing a historical account, and why I have sought to recount my adventures in anecdotal form.

Some of my grandchildren may wonder why I often adopt a faintly derisive tone when referring to a literary giant like André Malraux. I mean no offence, because I admired him immensely, but I was young at the time, and certain of his characteristics tickled my sense of humour. I should add that it was a godsend for the Resistance that men like Malraux should have joined us. They were few and far between, believe me. His personality, enthusiasm and contempt for danger made an important contribution to the Resistance and lent a new dimension to those who joined it. Whatever certain expert detractors may say, he was a true *résistant*.* I am proud of having joined the Resistance early on; Malraux did not become an activist until half-way through 1943, but so what?

Others of my grandchildren may wonder why I refer to Pétain with such hostility. It's true: I do, and my feelings for him have never changed.

Finally, *Grand-Père,* why the title? It sounds like a Disney nature film.

Read on, *mes enfants.* 'The giraffe has a long neck' was a coded message broadcast by '*Ici Londres*' on 4 June, 1944. It informed me that two days later we would emerge from the shadows, and that the dawn of freedom – your freedom – was breaking at last.

*English has no single word for 'member of the Resistance', so '*résistant*' will be used from now on.

THE JUMP

The door of the hut opened and Jacques Poirier, alias Lieutenant Jack Peters, alias Nestor, came out on to the apron of the RAF airfield near London.

It was raining, and the roar of aero engines made conversation futile. Encumbered by the parachute on his back, Jacques made his way over to the aircraft feeling slightly bemused and ill at ease. Waiting for him under the wing with several other officers, all of whom looked chilled to the bone, was Colonel Maurice Buckmaster, head of the French section of SOE*. He shook Jacques by the hand.

'On behalf of the Allies, I'd like to present you with this little gift.'

He proffered a handsome silver cigarette case, then came to attention and saluted smartly.

'*Merci* and good luck, old boy.'

Jacques was too constricted by his parachute harness to return the salute. He scrambled into the aircraft as best he could.

The freight compartment was almost empty. No seats, just a few containers. Jacques sat down on the floor. Just then he caught sight of another figure seated on the floor like himself – a rather delicate-looking young man. The pilot came aft to introduce himself and give them some information about the flight. When

*Special Operations Executive. An account of its role and functions will be found on p.53

3

they reached the French coast, he said, he would go into a steep dive and fly at zero feet to avoid the anti-aircraft fire.

'Don't worry,' he told them modestly, 'you're in luck. We're the top RAF crew for this type of mission.'

Jacques reviewed his last few days in England as the aircraft gathered speed and took off. Having completed his training nearly three weeks before, he had been waiting to leave for France ever since. This wasn't his first visit to the airfield. Two weeks ago they had actually been helping him into his flying suit when, for some unknown reason, the flight was cancelled and they sent him back to his London hotel. Three days later he was told to get ready to leave for the coast – arrangements had been made to land him by submarine, but that mission was cancelled too. The effect of all these vicissitudes had been to steel his nerves and endow him with a phlegmatic disposition worthy of the Englishman he would later impersonate. Consequently, he had displayed little emotion when the message reached him on the eve of this third attempt: 'It's any moment now, so stay on your toes and don't budge from the hotel.'

He stayed put all day long. Half-suspecting another false alarm, however, he had been imprudent enough (he was only twenty-one) to fix a dinner date with a charming young English girl in the WRNS. He had met her a few days before, but had not breathed a word about his military activities for reasons of security.

At five p.m. came another message warning him to be ready: a car would pick him up that evening. He had packed his bag and left the hotel without informing his girlfriend, who would by now be wondering what had become of her dinner date.

On arrival at the airfield he was promptly taken to a small hut, where he had a hurried evening meal and underwent a thorough inspection. They re-examined his suit, cut *à la française* by a London tailor working for the SOE, and ensured that the label of a French tailor was firmly sewn into it. They also examined his pockets in case they harboured a stray London Underground ticket. He was issued with some French money and a number of documents: forged identity card, driver's licence, ration card, and a few letters and photos calculated to deceive the enemy. Finally, he had put on a flying suit over his clothes, taken his parachute, said goodbye to Colonel

Buckmaster, and . . . that was as far as he got before he dozed off.

He was woken by a friendly tap on the shoulder.

'Not long now!' the dispatcher yelled.

He opened the central hatch and gestured to Jacques to sit down beside it with his legs almost dangling in space. His young fellow passenger followed suit on the other side. The dispatcher checked the webbing that connected the parachutes to the aircraft.

'See that little red light up there? When it goes green, jump!'

The plane banked. Jacques peered into the gloom, trying to make out Montignac en Dordogne. Their scheduled landing site was three kilometres north-east of the town. Henri Peulevé would be waiting down there with his reception committee. Jacques felt his heart beat faster. He was ready for action.

The two young parachutists sat there uncomfortably for ten long minutes. Jacques began to wonder if he would find himself back in London yet again. He was briefly considering whether to jump without waiting for the green light – 'I'll manage,' he told himself – when the engines slowed. He saw the dispatcher gesticulate and heard him shout 'Get ready!' Then, just as the little green light overhead came on, he heard 'Go!' and jumped.

The chill air filled his lungs, the roar of the engines and the whistle of the wind smote his ears. Then the parachute opened with a crack and silence fell. He could see the shadowy ground and, more to the point, a river that seemed to be coming up to meet him at an alarming speed. Would he miss it? He landed abruptly on the bank, one foot in the water, the other in the mud, and quickly scrambled on to firmer ground. He had the unpleasant impression, as he extricated himself from his parachute, that he hadn't landed where he was expected to land. The river didn't appear on the map he had so carefully studied at the offices of the SOE. The silence was unbroken. Cautiously, he made his way through the darkness. No one around. He wondered what had become of his young companion. He was just stowing his parachute behind a clump of bushes when he heard noises – shouts, even. He concealed himself in the undergrowth as best he could, drew the commando knife from his flying suit, and waited.

Footsteps were approaching. He could hear voices – French voices, a positive babble of them. Everyone was talking at once.

'I saw a parachutist coming down, I tell you!'

'Nonsense! Either you imagined it, or it was an arms drop. We'd better find the containers.'

Another voice: 'Yes, let's pick them up fast.'

'It's us who'll get picked up if we stay here much longer.'

'Shut your trap, you Pétainist!'

'Same to you, you Communist! You sang a different song in 1940!'

Jacques Poirier decided that it would be safe to make his presence known. The men promptly stopped talking and gesticulating. They stared in disbelief at the self-assured youngster advancing on them with a knife in his hand.

'What did I tell you!' said the first voice. 'It's an Englishman!'

Well, why not? thought Jacques. Perhaps it really would be better to pass himself off as an Englishman. At least they wouldn't insist on knowing where he stood politically. You didn't discuss politics with an 'Anglais'. And that was how, on returning to his beloved France, Lieutenant Jacques Poirier, alias Peters or Nestor, became 'Jack l'Anglais'.

His fellow passenger was discovered not far away. They learned that the pilot of their aircraft had dropped them some hundred kilometres from the prearranged spot.

I
TIME FOR TEARS: 1940

Cannes was enjoying a spell of glorious weather in June, 1940. The Croisette seemed to sparkle like a jewel in the sunlight, which was already hot for the time of year.

The promenade teemed with people. Those who had been lucky enough to find deck-chairs were serenely roasting in the sun. The sea was pleasantly warm for the beginning of the holiday season. Pretty girls scampered along the beach or splashed and giggled in the water, simultaneously making sure that they were being watched. Anyone ignorant of current events would have been surprised to learn that this peaceful, cheerful scene was set in a country on the brink of an abyss and only days away from sustaining one of the most grievous military defeats in its history.

The army of the King of the Belgians had surrendered barely ten days ago; elements of the French and British armies, cut off by the Germans' armoured hammer-blows, were embarking at Dunkirk; a terrible battle was developing on the Somme and the Aisne; and here, only a few kilometres from the Croisette, Mussolini was preparing to stab his fellow Latins in the back.

Alain and I walked fast, hardly sparing a glance for the frolicking water nymphs.

'They're working on their tan,' Alain muttered. 'For when the Italians get here.'

'If that bastard Mussolini crosses the frontier,' I said fiercely, 'I'll chuck college and join up.'

Alain slowed down, then paused to get his breath back. His asthma was giving him trouble.

'We're not even eighteen yet. You honestly think our parents would let us join up?' He drew another deep breath and smiled. 'Meantime, if we don't get to Boulevard Carnot in the next ten minutes, we can kiss those driving licences goodbye.'

9

His apt reminder quelled my warlike ardour. I had become convinced that a driving licence would be indispensable, what with the war and my father being in the forces, and was confident of passing the test. I had been driving for a long time. My father, an air force officer, often allowed me to drive the old Citroën B2 van which he kept in the grounds of Saint-Cyr, near Versailles. Our age was the problem. In view of the situation, would the inspector shut his eyes to the fact that we were a few weeks short of eighteen? He was waiting for us. He examined our papers and listened to our explanations, seeming quite as preoccupied with current developments as we were, then made me take the wheel of his car. Ten minutes later Alain and I had our licences.

Alain's lodgings were near Boulevard Carnot, so he left me there and I made my way up to our temporary home at Le Cannet, above Cannes.

In normal times we lived at Neuilly, just outside Paris, where I was born and had embarked on my studies at the Lycée Pasteur. My father was an extremely active, dynamic man who pursued two parallel careers, one to do with flying, the other with motor cars. Having been a pilot during the 1914–18 war, he was recalled to the air force in 1938. He had then decided that my mother and we two youngsters would be better off on the Côte d'Azur than in Paris during his absence, especially if war broke out.

I always enjoyed hearing the story of his marriage to my mother. He often got a chance to visit Paris during the 1914–18 war, and his train used to stop for a few minutes at Saint-Michel-sur-Orge. Noticing a girl at the window of a house opposite the station there, he gained the impression that she was smiling at him. That was how, one day, he came to get off the train and, in consequence, marry my mother.

It wasn't as simple as it sounds, of course, because the girl's parents already had two flyers in the family, their son and the fiancé of another of their daughters. They resigned themselves to the arrival of a third aviator with little enthusiasm and insisted that my father renounce his dangerous activities as soon as the war was over. 'It's an insane occupation,' was his mother-in-law's considered opinion.

Rather than lose his beloved, my father duly promised to give up flying. Once the war was over he did so and became, of all things, a racing driver. He competed at Le Mans, Spa, San Sebastián, and elsewhere. Some years later, doubtless with his mother-in-law's consent, he abandoned motor racing and reverted to flying. He took advantage of this dispensation to fly himself and his little family all over the place. By the time we were thirteen or fourteen, my brother Raymond and I must have put in more flying hours than all our fellow students at the Lycée Pasteur combined.

I got to Le Cannet at last and took the stairs two at a time, itching to share the news of my success with my mother and Raymond. Bursting into the apartment, I found myself face to face with my father. He gave me a hug and announced that we were leaving at once for Bordeaux.

'I've got a thirty-six-hour pass,' he told me. 'Mussolini's going to declare war on us, and I don't want my family caught up in the fighting while I'm elsewhere. I'll have time to drive you to our friends the Martins at Bordeaux and rejoin my squadron at Tours.'

I was dumbfounded. 'But I don't want to leave,' I began angrily, 'and if the Italians walk in . . .'

My father cut me short. 'I know how you feel, but I'm on active service and I don't know when I'll be back. While I'm gone, your first duty is to take care of your mother and Raymond. I'll be a lot easier in my mind if I know you're with friends in Bordeaux.'

So the Poirier family set off for Bordeaux. Not that my father could have known it, the Italian army never entered Cannes in June, 1940. Instead, Pétain sued for peace and Bordeaux was occupied by the Germans!

Monsieur Martin, one of my father's fellow flyers in the 1914–18 war, had also been recalled to the colours, leaving his wife Hélène in sole charge of the household. It was a sizeable establishment, because she had five children of widely varying ages, the two eldest, Jacqueline and Monique, being contemporaries of my brother's and mine. She also looked after her adoptive mother, who was the widow of the famous composer Saint-Saëns.

Hélène Martin was an exceptional woman who had the knack of combining authority with hospitality. She decided after a few days that we would all be more comfortable in her family's villa at Pyla, near Arcachon.

Then came the morning when the Germans entered Pyla. I would be eighteen next month. I had no idea where my father was. For all I knew, he had flown off to North Africa.

The house was silent, but from my room I seemed to hear muffled sounds in the distance. No, I told myself, it must be my imagination. Raymond, sensing my uneasiness, gave me a look of mild inquiry. I shivered involuntarily. Why were we all here? Simply because our fathers, who had been mobilized and parted from us, preferred their families to be together at such a difficult time. A creditable, consoling sentiment in two veterans of the last war, granted, but what was I going to do instead of fighting? Study for admission to the air force academy, as arranged, when my country was occupied by the Boches?

This time there was no mistake. I could hear the medley of sounds quite distinctly. It was growing louder, drawing nearer: a mechanical hum overlaid with the strains of a brass band. I jumped up and ran down the stairs four at a time. In the hallway I bumped into Monique, the Martins' eldest daughter and a special friend of mine. We stared at each other. Raymond had caught me up by this time, and the three of us hurried outside. I could hear my mother calling, 'Jacques, children, come back!'

We sprinted down the street to the boulevard. Five or six youngsters of our own age had already gathered there. Tears filled our eyes as the Germans paraded past. We felt crushed, frozen with horror. All at once, someone – it could have been anyone, even me – started singing, diffidently at first, then with growing assurance.

'Allons, enfants de la patrie . . .'

No longer a mere handful, our choir soon swelled to a score or more. We sang the *Marseillaise* with fervour, sending its vibrant message of hope across the boulevard. The Boches continued to march past without so much as a glance in our direction. They were ignoring us, the swine; to them we were merely children. I did, however, catch the eye of one youth in field-grey who must have been my own age.

I felt a hand on my shoulder. It was my mother. She and Hélène Martin were both in tears.

'I beg you, children, let's go home.'

I had yet to learn the meaning of the term '*résistant*', but I realized much later that it was then, at Pyla, that I became one. Some days after this incident I happened to hear a French general broadcasting from London. The reception was too poor for me to make out every word he said, but I got the gist of his message. The immense determination and confidence which General de Gaulle conveyed that day were never to leave me throughout the war. Whatever means we employed in taking the road he mapped out for us, he and France were indissolubly linked in my mind from then on.

I and my family were in a bizarre situation, that much was obvious. We lived at Cannes, which was in the unoccupied zone, but had inadvertently put our heads in the lion's jaws by moving to the south-west, an area under German occupation. My father, who had been posted to our embassy in Madrid while Marshal Pétain was still ambassador, was marooned there and waiting to return to France.

Early in August my mother asked me if I felt competent to drive our car from Pyla to Cannes.

'I think we should try to go back.'

I told her I foresaw no problem in driving the old Delage, but she hesitated. To leave the occupied zone we would need a permit from the *Kommandantur*, and she was reluctant to approach the German authorities. Raymond and I grew impatient, so she finally swallowed her pride and did so. Since she could prove that she was resident in the unoccupied zone, authorization was swiftly granted. Having said goodbye to the Martins, a procedure involving hugs and kisses all round, we retraced our route to Cannes, this time with me at the wheel.

Discounting the Martin family, I had spent little time in the company of my compatriots during our stay in the south-west. With the naïvety of an eighteen-year-old, I took it for granted that their reaction to the armistice must be the same as mine – that they were all on the side of General de Gaulle, at least in spirit – because I found it unimaginable that Frenchmen could tolerate foreign invaders on their soil.

I was sorely mistaken. On returning to Cannes I found, to my profound sorrow and disappointment, that many members of the population were going about their business as usual, intent on their petty, everyday concerns, and that the only perceptible consequence of our defeat seemed to be a preoccupation with the problem of food supplies.

It has to be said that the Côte d'Azur produced few vegetables at this time. Far from its principal sources of supply, hampered by lack of transport, and faced with a massive influx of refugees, it was probably subject to greater shortages than other regions during 1940 and 1941.

What was more serious, the Pétain government laid the blame for our defeat on others. Delighted to be absolved of responsibility for it, many French people seized on this explanation with alacrity. Who else were to blame but the British, the freemasons, and – of course – the Jews? General de Gaulle was a traitor! What distressed me most of all was to see so many veterans, men who had acquitted themselves nobly in the First World War, rush to answer Pétain's summons and parade down rue d'Antibes as if we had just won a major battle. It was pathetic, the extent to which hypocritical propaganda could mislead perfectly honourable citizens and distort their emotions. If Pétain's name had been Dupont, would we have seen these deplorable parades, which paved the way for the formation of the [fascist] Légion and the Milice?

Even today I feel incensed when I hear Pétain's apologists seeking to excuse the man who almost robbed us of our honour for ever. How many Frenchmen would have collaborated with the enemy if Laval had been in sole charge? Wrapped in the lingering aura of his First World War victories and lavishly rewarded by the republic he detested, Pétain abused his fellow countrymen. But for him, we should not have to blush at the memory of this period. He 'made France the gift of his person', to quote his own words – yes, but he did so by abasing himself before the enemy.

It is obvious that not all my compatriots were indifferent, exclusively preoccupied with their bellies, or ready to engage in what became known as collaboration. I encountered a few who believed that we must soon do something to carry on the war. Ideas on the subject were vague, just as the Resistance itself was locally unknown. Sneak off to England? Easier said than done. Words still predominated over deeds, but our often heated discussions welded us together and taught us a great deal. I got to know all kinds of people at this period: middle-class youths like myself, anarchists, manual workers, Cagoulard revolutionaries, royalists, socialists, republicans, right- and left-wing extremists. For all our differences, we formed a united group whose common denominator was a determination to expel the invader.

Nineteen forty-one was well under way. The Pétainists were preparing to embark on collaboration by setting up institutions dedicated to the New Order, but a growing number of my fellow countrymen, though initially influenced by Vichy, had seen the light and taken refuge in eloquent silence. The ingenuity with which they coped with shortages of food and clothing was marvellous to behold.

The family had insisted that I continue my studies, but my thoughts were elsewhere. I and my little circle of associates were forever forging new plans, some of which came within an ace of succeeding.

Together with three of our friends, Alain and I had discovered a motor launch in the harbour at Cannes which seemed to be in perfect condition. Nobody ever went aboard, so we decided to risk paying it a visit. Alain, a first-class mechanic, inspected the engine and pronounced it in good working order. One thing led to another, and we started to make more concrete plans, one of them being to procure some petrol and transport it aboard in dribs and drabs. Our idea, harebrained though it was, was to head for Gibraltar in the hope of being picked up by a British ship well short of the Rock. It was a crazy scheme, and our chances of success were slender because the harbour mouth was under close surveillance, but we spent a long time working on this operation. Night after night we crept aboard with instalments of food and fuel and I even purloined an aircraft compass belonging to my father. Our friends, doubtless for very sound reasons, backed out one by one as the days went by, until only Alain and I were left. In the end, even we realized that we were flogging a dead horse, and the motor launch remained at its moorings.

On another occasion my father announced that he and some other airmen were going to try to reach England in a seaplane hidden on the Étang-de-Berre, a lagoon to the west of Marseilles, and promised to take me with them. This scheme, too, was abandoned, but it was a genuine project organized by officers of the French air force.

II
THE AWAKENING

It was not until the end of 1941 that I managed to establish a really interesting contact – one that introduced me, by degrees, into a genuine resistance movement.

My parents had moved to a house near Mougins. This was inconvenient from my own point of view, because I had to keep making the round trip to Cannes, where all my friends and fellow 'conspirators' were based. It was nevertheless at Mougins, and in a wholly fortuitous manner, that the doors of the Resistance finally opened to me.

The Missons were some charming neighbours of ours. Monsieur Misson seemed to spend most of his time tending the flowers in his garden. While chatting with him one afternoon I must have made my feelings pretty plain and intimated that I wanted to go into action against the invader. He made no comment, but a few days later, after a few innocuous remarks, he became more explicit.

'You know, Jacques,' he said, very deliberately, 'if one wants to do something useful these days, it's better not to talk too much.'

He dispelled my alarm with a reassuring smile. Then, drawing my attention to some superb roses, he added, 'If you're interested, I think I can help you.'

That was the last I saw of Monsieur Misson for a couple of weeks. I lay in wait, hoping to catch sight of him in his garden, but without success. Then, one morning, he reappeared and asked if I would like to run down to Cannes with him. We mounted our motorized push-bikes and I followed in his wake. He pulled up in Boulevard Carnot, just beyond the Collège de Cannes. A man was waiting for us.

'Jacques,' said Monsieur Misson, 'this is Romano.' So saying, he promptly puttered off.

Romano was a frail, mournful-looking southerner, but his voice, when he spoke with the singsong intonation of the Midi, was firm and resolute. He suggested taking a few minutes' stroll along the boulevard. Without preamble, he subjected me to a thorough interrogation, concentrating on my previous history and gauging my reaction to his questions, some of which were indiscreet. I got the impression that he was satisfied with my replies, because, after ten minutes, he began to explain the nature and objectives of his organization, whose name he carefully refrained from disclosing.

'We can't do too many things at once,' he told me. 'Our job is to get ready for the day when we and our allies are able to drive the enemy out. At present we need a smart, resourceful fellow who can keep his mouth shut – a courier willing to deliver pamphlets and other printed matter. It's risky, but I've a feeling you're the man for the job.' As if he'd already said too much, he concluded curtly, 'All right, that's it. Misson will let you know my decision. Don't forget: the Resistance is still in its infancy. For the moment, don't trust another living soul.' And he walked off.

That was how, a few days later, I joined the Resistance. I think I was working for the 'Combat' movement, but I'm not entirely sure; no one ever told me.

After some weeks Romano asked me to move to Cannes, so I left Mougins and moved into a small boarding-house of his choosing. It was no palace, and although my rent was paid by the Resistance I had very little money in my pocket.

Romano kept me pretty busy, but I seldom reflected on the dangers of my job. I delivered messages to all parts of the town and its environs, often carrying clandestine pamphlets and leaflets that would undoubtedly have spelled a prison sentence if the police had stopped me. I had become the perfect errand boy. I did weigh up the risks sometimes. On one occasion I was asked to take a package from La Bocca to Boulevard de la République in Cannes on my motor-assisted push-bike. On picking it up at La Bocca I glimpsed enough of the contents to realize that it was a radio transmitter. Securing it to the rack in front of my handlebars, I blithely set off for Cannes. All at once, as I rounded a bend, I caught sight of a group of men in civilian clothes wearing arm-bands – probably members of Marshal Pétain's *Légion*. They were busy setting up a road-block. It was too late to turn back, so I kept going. I slowed, ostensibly to indicate my intention of stopping. Then, when I was almost on top of them, I abruptly accelerated. Shouts rang out.

'Stop! What are you up to? What's that you've got there?'

But I was already past them and out of reach. My heart thudded against my ribs. I'd made it. I continued on my way, feeling not a little proud of myself.

'Where are the fuses?' Romano demanded when I delivered the transmitter. 'How do you expect this contraption to work without any fuses? You'll have to go back and get them.'

'Not today,' I told him, calmly but firmly.

Another time, Romano announced that I was going to meet *le Capitaine*. 'He wants to see you. He's the boss.'

Shortly afterwards I found myself in an apartment on Boulevard Carnot. (I went there so often I began to wonder if the entire street was given over to the Resistance.) The boss was a formidable-looking man with a luxuriant thatch of snow-white hair. He told me that we would soon be entering a much more active phase, and that I was now to start recruiting some really staunch and reliable friends. When I asked him if I couldn't join de Gaulle in London, he turned snappish.

'I just got back,' he said curtly. 'You'd be wasting your time. It's all in-fighting and politics over there. The real battle is here. If you want to serve your country you must remain in France.'

I left a few minutes later, rather disconcerted, I must confess. Although I knew what had to be done in France, I failed at that time to grasp the potential scope of our task, particularly in an environment rendered hostile by Pétain's policy, and felt that I could make a greater contribution as a member of a properly constituted army based in England. That said, I quickly set to work. Together with some friends of my own age, I gradually built up a small but resolute group of activists, several of them girls.

One day, looking more lugubrious than ever, Romano announced that he was going to entrust me with a very tricky, top secret mission.

'Do you speak English?' he asked.

Impressed by my affirmative response, which was, to be frank, a gross exaggeration, he told me that a British officer had landed by parachute, but had unfortunately broken his leg in the process.

'We've been hiding him at a friend's place in Mougins, but his leg is better and he wants to carry out his mission as soon as possible. For that he'll need an efficient sidekick, and I think you'll fill the bill.'

That was how I first encountered Henri Peulevé. It was a meeting destined to have a crucial influence on my Resistance activities.

Henri Peulevé, a British major aged around thirty, was Huguenot by origin, hence his un-English name. He had lived near Menton for several years before the war, and his French was excellent. Henri radiated charm, humour and confidence. He was also a man of decision and authority. Despite the difference in our ages, it took us only a few hours to become friends.

Discounting my own little group and Romano, I had had little contact with other members of the Resistance before meeting Henri. Monsieur Misson's warning had sunk in. I felt that discretion was essential if my missions were to be guaranteed maximum security, and so, except when meeting them in the course of my work, I had avoided becoming friendly with other *résistants*. Henri's presence in Cannes changed all that, because many incautious souls who had heard of the Englishman's arrival were eager to meet him. Indeed, I was absolutely appalled by their lack of discretion. One evening, when I turned up at the Café de la Régence for a prearranged meeting with Henri, I asked one of the regulars if he had seen him.

'The Englishman?' he said loudly. 'He's over there with some friends.'

I was furious. 'If you carry on like this,' I told Henri later, 'you'll wind up behind bars in double-quick time, and so will I.'

Henri promptly conceded the point but excused himself by arguing that it was difficult to offend decent folk.

'What do you expect?' he said. 'They've got themselves a tame Englishman and they want to show him off. After all, it's good for morale.'

'Morale be damned,' I told him. 'We'll put a stop to all this. You're coming to Beaulieu. My parents have just moved there. That way, you'll be incommunicado.'

I learned a lot at this period about the objectives of the Allies and General de Gaulle in regard to the Resistance. Henri explained that it would become a formidable weapon only if, by the time the Allies landed in Europe, it had developed into a genuine fighting force capable of contributing to final victory by severing the enemy's lines of communication.

'We believe,' he told me, 'that the Resistance must preserve itself intact for D-Day. Any rash moves, any premature uprisings, and all we'll find when we land is a *résistants'* graveyard. That doesn't mean you can't get organized as of now, or carry out selective operations and acts of sabotage designed to erode the enemy's morale and his defensive capability on D-Day.'

Henri, who had established radio contact with London, announced that he had just received orders to return to England. I was a trifle disappointed, knowing that I was in a position to do far more effective work with him than in my own group. Reading my thoughts, Henri reassured me by saying that he had passed my name to London and that, from now on, I was an accepted member of his organization. The only thing was, I would have to accompany him to London to undergo a course of training. I had no precise idea of the nature of his organization, but I was thrilled at the prospect of joining the Allies in London – thrilled and, I must confess, highly flattered to have been selected. Henri blandly inquired if I approved of the plan. I told him I did.

I went to Romano and explained my problem. He seemed delighted.

'Jacques,' he said warmly, 'that's terrific. You've won your spurs and moved up a rung. I'm very proud of you. You're one of the bosses now, and I've every confidence in you. Lots of luck.'

I gave him the name of the person in my group best qualified to replace me. Romano was a true *résistant*, a decent, courageous man, and I regretted having to bid him farewell.

My brother Raymond undertook to inform Serge Bouder, the person I had appointed to succeed me. Serge did not, unfortunately, last long in the job. He was arrested, interned, and subsequently deported to Germany. While on the way there he managed to escape by jumping from a moving train and thus avoided ending up in a death camp.

Thanks to an untoward combination of circumstances, Henri and I were just preparing to leave for England when the French fleet was scuttled at Toulon and the Germans marched into the unoccupied zone. There could not have been a worse time to embark on such a journey. Our plans had not allowed for the possibility that our navy might present the free world with such a deplorable spectacle.

Our organization had given us the name of a priest in Marseilles who would make arrangements for us to travel via Spain, so we duly took a train to Marseilles. It was not a pleasant trip. The Toulon sinkings and the invasion of the unoccupied zone had created a very uneasy atmosphere, and our papers were examined at least five times en route. Each such occasion was particularly tricky for Henri, whose false papers and slight accent might have alerted some over-zealous policeman. When we stopped at Toulon station we could still see smoke rising above the harbour, doubtless from the last of the scuttled ships. One could only imagine how much those magnificent vessels might have meant to France and her allies if only their crews had done their duty and headed out to sea.

We found our contact, Abbé Winter, after making a few inquiries. He was very suspicious of us, even though we gave him the prearranged password, and remained extremely wary. In the end he told us that he was being closely watched, and that we would be better advised, for our personal safety's sake, to move on as soon as possible. Just as we were leaving, however, he apologized for being unable to help us himself and recommended a professional smuggler based at Perpignan – a 'thoroughly reliable type'.

We boarded a train for Perpignan, our journey made no more agreeable by the growing frequency with which we sighted German uniforms. On arrival we had no difficulty in finding the smuggler, who quickly agreed to guide us into Spain.

'We'll leave tomorrow,' he said. He added that smuggling had become a great deal more hazardous since the Germans moved into the unoccupied zone. This being so, he would have to double his fee.

This came as a shock to us. Although Henri had some money on him, he didn't have enough left to meet our smuggler's requirements. The man grasped our difficulty at once and suggested that we check into a small hotel he knew.

'Perhaps we'll be able to solve your problem there,' he told us.

We followed him to the hotel and entered the lobby.

'I'm off now,' he said calmly, 'but I'll be back in a couple of hours. See that family sitting in the corner? They're Jews. They're also leaving tomorrow. Have a word with them. Maybe they'll help you out.' So saying, he left us.

I was feeling very disillusioned. I had thought I belonged to an organization capable of getting us into Spain as smoothly and efficiently as Thomas Cook. Far from it: not only did the smuggler expect a fat fee, but unless we came up with the money by tomorrow we wouldn't get away at all. Henri read my thoughts as usual.

'I may have the answer,' he said. 'They told me in London that if I ever needed money I was authorized to borrow it from private individuals on the Treasury's behalf. All I have to do is to get the people in question to think up a message. I pass it on to London, and if the BBC transmits it the same night they've got a deal, QED!'

I was flabbergasted.

'You really think you can waltz up to someone in the lobby of a hotel swarming with Germans and police, and say: "I'm a British officer. I need some money, and if you care to give me a message. . . ."' I paused. 'Anyway, how do you propose to contact London by tonight? Where's your radio?'

'That's just the trouble,' Henri said, straight-faced, 'but I don't have any choice.'

Under other circumstances a private individual might have felt pretty certain that everything was above-board if he received a message from the BBC. Lending money to a British agent would be his personal contribution to the Allied war effort, and he could hope to cut a truly heroic figure when the Treasury repaid him after the war. Our situation was altogether different, but Henri, with colossal cheek, accosted the strangers at the corner table and performed the necessary miracle. Although the Jewish paterfamilias realized that there was no prospect of his hearing a message from the BBC in the immediate future, he courageously accepted Henri's proposal and lent us the money we needed.

I think it worth mentioning that the refugees in question escaped to Spain some days later and were reimbursed, soon after the Liberation, by the British government.

Our smuggler returned to the hotel, pocketed a down payment, and arranged to meet us again the next day.

III
THE JOURNEY

Crossing the Pyrenees

At ten the next morning our smuggler turned up at the hotel, accompanied by a friend, and showed us where to catch the bus to Céret.

'Be very careful,' he told us. 'The bus passes near the frontier, so it's closely watched. There'll be frequent police checks. I'll be on board myself, but don't speak to me. I'll tip you the wink when it's time to get off.'

He inspected our peasant outfits and seemed satisfied with them.

When we boarded the bus several hours later I noticed that the Jewish refugees were already seated at the back. This was a nuisance, because the poor people would undoubtedly slow us down. The smuggler hadn't mentioned that they would be coming too; on the contrary, he had assured us that we would be going across on our own. We joined them at the back of the vehicle, which lumbered off.

We had been travelling towards Céret along a minor road for some twenty minutes when the bus came to an abrupt stop and three gendarmes got in.

'Police check!' barked one of them. 'Papers!'

He returned Henri's forged documents without a word, took my genuine identity card and studied it thoughtfully for several seconds, then stared at me with an ominous look in his eye. I had begun to fear the worst when he suddenly noticed that his two colleagues had completed their inspection, handed back my papers, and made for the door. I felt abnormally hot for the time of year!

We had been travelling for at least three hours when our guide, who was comfortably ensconced near the driver, gave us a surreptitious signal. The bus pulled up soon afterwards and we and the Jewish family got out.

We were in the middle of nowhere. Now we would start the long ascent – or so I thought. After we had been walking for a good hour the guide came to a halt.

'Take it easy for a bit,' he said. 'I'm going on ahead with my friend to see if the coast is clear. We'll be back in five minutes.'

Henri and I took advantage of this respite to have a bite to eat. The Jewish family did likewise. They were all in good shape except the mother, who was already looking tired but doing her best not to show it. Ten minutes went by, then half an hour. It became clear that our guide and his companion had simply abandoned us on this mountain track. It was an unenviable situation. What should we do, press on or return to Perpignan? We quickly realized that we couldn't cross the mountains on our own. We had no map, no compass. All we could do was try to get back to Perpignan.

Having spent an uncomfortable night in the open, we made the return journey by bus in an apprehensive, dejected frame of mind. It was a relatively uneventful trip. Our Jewish friends bade us farewell.

'Don't worry about us,' the father said. 'We know where to go.'

Henri and I had only one course open to us: to return to Marseilles and demand an explanation from Abbé Winter. We would have to economize, though, because our exchequer was badly depleted.

We were tired and beginning to feel hungry, but we decided to go straight to the station and catch the next train to Marseilles. We had been waiting on the platform for some minutes when I suddenly spotted our smuggler and his confederate standing with their backs to us on the adjoining platform, waiting for a train in the opposite direction. I signalled to Henri, and without stopping to think we hared over to the two swindlers and sneaked up behind them. I was wearing an old lumber-jacket. Burying my right hand in one of the capacious pockets, I jabbed my forefinger firmly into the smuggler's back.

30

'Not a sound,' I heard myself say, very quietly. 'We're leaving together. One false move and you're a dead man.'

From one moment to the next, to my own vast surprise, I had become a thug. Henri was crowding the smuggler's accomplice in an equally menacing manner. The two men were utterly thunderstruck. Beside themselves with fear, they preceded us into the street.

'What do you want?' the smuggler asked. 'I'll give you back your money.'

'No,' said Henri, 'you're going to guide us into Spain right away.'

'Impossible,' said the man, 'there isn't another bus till this afternoon.'

'That's fine with us,' I put in. 'We're starving. I spotted a black market restaurant just up the road. Nice of you to invite us to lunch.'

They sat between us in the restaurant, unable to swallow a morsel. As for Henri and me, we shamelessly went through the menu and washed the meal down with liberal quantities of wine. The smuggler settled the bill and accompanied us to the bus, still trembling. I wedged myself in beside him with Henri seated beside his confederate immediately in front of us.

Crossing the Pyrenees in November was an unpleasant experience. It was cold, and we encountered snow as we climbed. Henri's leg, which had only just recovered from the fracture he had sustained when parachuting into France, pained him terribly, and he often had to lean on me. The guides had got over their fear and set a brisk pace. Being in their element, they realized that the boot was now on the other foot. This time, however, they kept their part of the bargain, or at least the part that mattered. We walked for most of the night. Then, at about four in the morning, they halted and announced that we were in Spain at last.

'Have a rest. We'll go and fetch the Spanish guide.'

They didn't fool us a second time, but what was the use of arguing? We were in Spain.

'Let's take a breather,' Henri said. 'We'll work something out in due course.'

We realized after an hour that the Spanish guide wasn't

coming. It was rumoured that the Spaniards sometimes turned French refugees over to the Germans, so we tore up our French papers. Henri decided to introduce himself to the authorities as a British officer, which was true enough, and I opted for Canadian nationality.

'I'll find it easier to pass for a French Canadian than an Oxford undergraduate,' I told him.

Once that minor problem had been sorted out we set off down the mountainside into Spain. Some time later we sighted a village. I thought it would be wiser to bypass the place, being so near the frontier, because we would certainly be spotted if we walked straight through, but Henri was exhausted. 'Sorry,' he said; he was going to look for an inn and rest up there for a bit, so we pressed on. Like many small Spanish villages, this one consisted of a single main street flanked by high walls forming a kind of long corridor. These walls protected the houses beyond them but made it impossible to branch off in either direction.

We soon spotted a bus parked beside the road. Henri's spirits revived at the sight, and he broke into a limping run.

'Everything's all right,' he called over his shoulder. 'We've got a little Spanish money. I'll give it to the driver and he can take us to Barcelona.'

I followed in his wake. We had almost reached the bus when I saw it was full of Spanish civil guards. I caught Henri by the sleeve.

'Beat it, quick! They're Guardia Civil – don't you see those "typewriters"* on their heads?'

We ran back up the street as fast as we could. The Spaniards were too surprised to react at first, but they quickly recovered and levelled their rifles. We had no choice but to surrender to the Spanish authorities.

An officer came up and asked to see our papers. We explained as best we could that we were escaped Allied officers and weren't carrying any. We had taken part in the Commando raid on Dieppe and wanted to rejoin our units in England. The officer, who appeared to understand, shook hands and told us we were in luck: the Spanish government had just

*The rigid black leather headgear of the Spanish Civil Guard was oddly reminiscent of a typewriter.

come to an arrangement with the British embassy. By virtue of this, it would be his duty to escort us either to the embassy or to the nearest consulate. His entire speech was couched in excellent French. Henri was jubilant.

'*Magnifico!*' he exclaimed. '*Señor,* before you take us to the consulate, allow me to stand you a good meal!'

'*De acuerdo,*' the officer replied. 'I have some business to attend to in the village. Make yourself at home in the bus. On my return I shall take you to a hotel where we can have a good dinner and spend the night. Tomorrow morning you will be escorted to Barcelona.'

'*Viva España!*' I cried exultantly.

Later that day the officer returned with three colleagues. We boarded his personal conveyance, which resembled a jeep, and were driven to a small market town. Here we pulled up outside a charming inn. The officer conducted us to a room on the first floor and invited us to join him in the dining-room in half an hour.

Our Spanish escorts, who turned out to be a captain and three lieutenants, enjoyed an excellent dinner at the British government's expense. When Henri and I finally retired to the room we were sharing, we fell asleep at once. When I got up in the night, however, I cautiously opened the door and found myself face to face with two armed soldiers. We were obviously under guard.

I woke poor Henri and, half-asleep though we were, we held a council of war. What should we do? Any attempt to escape seemed fraught with danger, and the Spanish officers made an honest enough impression. There were soldiers outside our door, true, but that didn't mean the captain had been lying. Faintly perturbed but very weary, we went back to sleep.

Our Guardia Civil officers were as friendly as ever the next morning, and we headed for Barcelona in their company. We were driving through Figueras when the captain pulled up outside a large building.

'Get out for minute,' he said. 'The man at the door will take you upstairs to see the magistrate. It's only a minor formality. You'll have to surrender your pesetas, but don't worry. We'll wait for you out here.'

The little magistrate was waiting for us in his first-floor office.

'I must ask you to hand over your Spanish currency,' he said affably in French. 'I'll make out a receipt and the money will in due course be returned to you via your embassy.'

The little we had left was just about enough to buy two single tickets to Barcelona, but who cared? The magistrate handed us a receipt. Then, with a broad smile, he announced, 'Gentlemen, you're free!'

Henri and I hurried back downstairs to our friends in the Guardia Civil. They had disappeared. Three plainclothesmen strode up to us. One of them drew a revolver and shepherded us firmly into a car. And that was how we ended up in Figueras Prison.

I have often wondered why the Spaniards employed such a ruse in order to get us into prison. The most likely explanation is that by treating us well and leading us to believe that we were going to our embassy they dissuaded us from trying to escape. What was more, this method of detention virtually ensured that we had no time to notify the embassy or consulate of our arrival in Spain.

In Prison at Figueras

The prison was a big, square fortress with a watchtower at each corner. The prison proper, which was enclosed by an outer wall, housed the prisoners' cells. Situated in the middle of this main building was an inner courtyard hemmed in by a formidable wall that completely obstructed one's view of the outside world. One glance sufficed to convince us that our chances of breaking out were slender indeed.

The prison was guarded by soldiers. They seemed to concentrate on external surveillance, leaving it to the Spanish political prisoners to supervise the other inmates.

It must be remembered that the Spanish Civil War was not long over, and one could not escape the impression that half the country's inhabitants were keeping the other half behind bars. The political prisoners had drawn incredibly long sentences. It was not uncommon to meet inmates who had been sentenced to terms of fifty or even a hundred years.

I am reminded of the story of one political prisoner who had received three death sentences. He discovered a distant cousin close to the Franco regime, and his family went to see the man. After much palaver, the cousin managed to get one death sentence commuted. Our prisoner then remembered that he had been well acquainted in his youth with a priest who had recently been elevated to the episcopate. He wrote to him at once. The bishop remembered his old friend, made representations to the authorities, and was overjoyed after several months to hear that he had managed to get a second death sentence commuted. The prisoner was left with only one death sentence outstanding, but that was enough to spell his doom!

To the political prisoners at Figueras, the growing influx of refugees from France was manna from heaven. When asking them to keep an eye on us, the prison authorities had intimated that, if they did the job efficiently, their cooperation would be taken into account and might knock something off their sentences – a pretty backhanded promise, considering that some of the prisoners had been sentenced to a hundred years' imprisonment and might possibly hope for a reduction to eighty!

The authorities entrusted the supervision of common criminals and foreign detainees to political prisoners who, in a spirit of equality, sometimes put members of the two categories in the same cell. Most of the Republicans performed their supervisory duties with alacrity. They cherished a special hatred for the French, whose failure to come to their aid during the civil war they blamed for their defeat, so they treated us pretty badly. The Guardia Civil, being thoroughly pro-Franco, regarded us with equal detestation because, in their view, we had backed the Republicans.

Such was the atmosphere to which Henri and I were introduced on being imprisoned at Figueras. There were twenty of us in a cell undoubtedly designed for eight at the most. We slept on the floor, and the place was so crowded that it was impossible for us all to lie down at the same time. The cell was long but narrow. There was no furniture of any kind, and the only amenity was a hole in one corner.

We had only just begun to make the acquaintance of our fellow inmates when the door opened and a guard, pointing to Henri and me, called, '*Vengan, coños!*'

He hustled us outside and along a very narrow passage to the inner courtyard, where some twenty other prisoners were waiting. More guards converged on us, laughing. They made us strip to the waist, after which a medical orderly blithely vaccinated us all with the same needle. We were then herded into a small room with several showers at the back. Another medical orderly came up, told me to undress completely, and proceeded to shave off every hair on my body. I was shivering by this time – it was a cold day – but yet another orderly made me sit on a stool and shaved my head to the scalp. Once that was done, a guard shoved me in the back.

'*Dúchate, coño!*'

I got under the shower. The jets of icy water were needle-sharp, and I instinctively recoiled. The guard gave me another shove and I found myself under the icy water again. This torment continued for a good five minutes. All my companions underwent the same treatment.

Back in our cell once more, we completed the introductions that had been so rudely interrupted.

It so happened, at least to begin with, that all of us were refugees from France. Our number included a French air force general, a politician, a major in the spahis, an eminent pianist of Polish origin, a well-known radio commentator, a Renault factory worker, a school-teacher, and one or two students like me. I was surprised to discover that the social hierarchy prevailing outside prison operated here too, and that it was accepted without demur. Not for long, though. By degrees, a new hierarchy took shape as the days went by. Some of those at the top of the ladder retained their places with ease; others quickly cracked and made a precipitate descent to the rung where they belonged, which they should never have left in the first place. Still others, the ones at the bottom of the ladder, revealed their true worth and innate sense of duty, and it was not long before they joined those who knew how to inspire and lead men.

Life in the cell became organized. It had been agreed that each of us, in his own particular field, should share a little of his knowledge with the others. For my part, I know that my love of music derives from the lessons which our esteemed Polish pianist managed to impart without an instrument. Thanks to our spahi major's accounts of his life in the desert, we also learned a great deal about the hardships and privations a soldier has to endure.

The nights were an ordeal. The lack of space became tiring in the long run, so we invented a system to beat it. At nightfall those ranged along the left-hand wall stretched out while those on the right did their best to sleep sitting up; in the middle of the night we changed places.

The worst problem of all, however, was the hole in the corner of the cell. Some of our number could not bring themselves to use it and became genuinely ill in consequence. What with that and the putrid, revolting food, nearly all of us suffered from attacks of dysentery.

At about ten every morning the guards opened the cell doors and we were entitled to an hour's 'recreation' in the inner courtyard. We could stroll around, exchange news with the occupants of other cells and glean information about the course of the war. We were always hungry. With the few pesetas we managed to pick up here and there we were occasionally able to buy an orange or a piece of *turrón* (Spanish nougat) from the little canteen in the courtyard. Whenever I got an orange I happily devoured it peel and all.

Sundays were gala occasions. We were marched off to compulsory Mass in the chapel, where we sat through an interminable service attended by all the prison dignitaries: governor, head warder, et cetera. The Francoists had devised an excellent method of establishing a close relationship between their political beliefs and religion. They not only made us sing the Francoist anthem at the end of the service but, to ensure that we fully grasped the significance of this stirring osmosis, obliged us to sing it with our right arms raised in the fascist salute.

This gesture did not appeal to the prisoners, especially those who had escaped from France, and we soon found an answer to it: we raised our arms, to be sure, but splayed two fingers in the V-sign dear to Winston Churchill. Our little ruse did not go unnoticed for long. The warders spotted it and launched a veritable V-hunt in the middle of Mass. Although they had scant success, their activities did help to brighten the proceedings a little.

During one such Mass Henri played a dirty trick on me. The prisoner in front of us, who was rather too eager to please, was singing the Francoist anthem with his arm too rigidly extended for our taste. Henri, spotting the man's hat on the pew beside him, promptly grabbed it and hung it on his outstretched hand. I couldn't restrain myself and burst out laughing. That laugh earned me twenty-four hours in solitary.

After Sunday Mass we were privileged to lunch alfresco in the prison yard. This 'feeding-time at the zoo' was also attended by the prison authorities, who looked on as we shuffled towards the serving table in single file, bowls in hand, and received a dollop of putrid stew. I was invariably hungry, but one day, noticing that the helping I'd just been given was alive with maggots, I looked the warders straight in the eye and contemptuously tipped my stew on the ground. A prisoner behind me darted forward and scooped it into his bowl.

We were growing really impatient. It wasn't part of our plan, having got across the Pyrenees, to spend the rest of the war in a Spanish prison. Our primary mission was to reach England as soon as possible.

'I've simply got to contact the British embassy in Madrid,' Henri told me. 'It's high time London knew where we are.'

An opportunity presented itself, but it was fraught with danger. We were periodically summoned to the governor's office to be questioned, a procedure that never varied. We had to state our name, nationality, and reasons for having entered Spain by clandestine means. Then came the invariable question:

'Are you a communist?'

One afternoon I received another summons to the prison office. An interpreter was standing just behind the governor's chair. I had just replied, as usual, that I was a Canadian officer who had landed at Dieppe and was anxious to rejoin his unit. The interpreter was translating. All at once, looking at me intently, he half-raised his fist in the communist salute. The governor was too busy noting down my reply to look at me. On impulse, I quickly returned the interpreter's salute. The man smiled, and I began to regret my impulsive gesture, convinced that I had fallen into a trap. As soon as I returned to the cell I told Henri about the incident. Contrary to my expectations, he said I had been right to respond because it was time to take a few risks.

'After all,' he said fiercely, 'we can't just rot here for ever.'

A few days later, while we were taking our daily stroll in the prison yard, I caught sight of the interpreter. Unobtrusively, he sauntered up to me.

'Anything I can do for you, comrade?' he murmured, looking everywhere but in my direction.

'Yes,' I said promptly, 'you can post a letter for me.'

'Very well,' he replied. 'I'll see you tomorrow.'

I got hold of some paper and an envelope, and Henri wrote a letter to his embassy which I gave to my comrade interpreter the next day. He was as good as his word. Ten days later Henri and I were summoned to the prison office. The governor was looking furious. The man beside him introduced himself.

'I'm an attaché at the British embassy. I've come to find out if you're being treated correctly.'

Henri exploded into English. He said something like, 'I don't give a damn if you know whether or not we're being treated correctly. What I want is to get out of here. We're at war, or hadn't you noticed?'

The interview had got off on the wrong foot, but Henri calmed down a little and the attaché explained his problem.

'Relations with the Spanish authorities aren't easy, but I think I can promise you that, if you don't do anything stupid, you'll soon be out of here.' Looking at me strangely, he added, 'You'll be transferred to an internment camp exclusively reserved for officers. It'll be a lot more comfortable.'

The Camp at Jaraba

One morning some twenty of us were ordered to assemble in the prison yard at Figueras, where our personal belongings were returned. Roped together, we emerged from the prison gates. Then, flanked by an impressive number of guards, we were marched through the town. It was a long and unenjoyable walk, but we finally reached the goods yard and were put aboard a freight car. Although we were untied, the doors were carefully secured and a dozen or so guards travelled with us. The journey took two days. The train stopped frequently, on one occasion for at least eight hours outside Barcelona. We had nothing to eat, but we were so glad to have left Figueras that our spirits were relatively high.

We eventually pulled into the station at Zaragoza, where we were roped together again and loaded into trucks. The road through the mountains was tortuous in the extreme, and we were thrown around like crates of merchandise, but we reached our destination at last.

Jaraba, in the province of Zaragoza, was a small thermal spa notable for the geysers surrounding it, which sent piping hot water gushing from the bowels of the earth. The rugged mountains that enclosed the little town formed a natural barrier.

There were five or six hotels in Jaraba, all of them very well appointed thanks to the proximity of the numerous bathhouses where natural hot water flowed in abundance for the benefit of visitors taking a cure. The situation in 1942 was such that the visitors had disappeared, however, so the Spanish authorities decided to close the spa and turn it into an internment camp. Conversion was an easy matter. There was plenty of accommodation, and the natural barrier surrounding the camp dispensed with the need for any vast expenditure on security measures. Earmarked for foreign officers interned in Spain, the camp was taken over by the army.

Conditions at Jaraba were very different from those we had encountered at Figueras. We were housed in hotels, two or three to a room, and entitled to two baths a week. The food was adequate, and we could move freely about the town during daylight hours. It was paradise compared to Figueras, but after a week of euphoria our old preoccupations returned. None of us intended to sit out the war in a prison camp, however comfortable, and plans for escape began to germinate in our minds.

The British military attaché paid us a visit and succeeded in putting a damper on our determination to escape, at least temporarily. Apart from Henri, the camp contained several other British army officers including Denis Rake, who was appointed 'senior officer', and a peculiar individual named Major Le Chène. I joined them in conversation with the British military attaché, who came straight to the point.

'We're pursuing a long-term policy with the Spaniards,' he told us. 'Everything depends on their neutrality. We feel we're making progress as far as your release is concerned, but any blunders on your part would jeopardize what we've achieved to date. I can assure you,' he concluded, 'that any attempt to escape would be counterproductive. We shall get you out of here in due course. Meantime, I want your solemn undertaking not to try to escape.'

We were furious, but we gave him our word, with the proviso that it would remain good for one month only.

The days went by. What with our strolls through the town and the interesting discussions we had with our fellow prisoners, all of them so different but all so united in their devotion to a single cause, the liberation of our country and the defeat of the Nazis, time passed far more quickly than it had at Figueras. Our conversations sometimes took an amusing turn.

One day a young officer named Jean-Claude Servan-Schreiber mentioned a friend of his who had a French mother and an English father.

'It tickles me to think that he was such a confirmed antimilitarist that he chose British nationality to avoid having to do military service in France. He's in England. I wonder what sort of a face he's pulling right now, with England in the thick of the war!'

I was dumbfounded, because my parents had been friendly with an Anglo-French family whose son fitted Jean-Claude's description to a T. I had seen him a few times when I was ten or twelve years old.

'I know who you mean,' I said calmly. 'It's George Hiller.'

This time it was Jean-Claude's turn to look dumbfounded.

But that's not the end of the story. George Hiller, subsequently Major Hiller, DSO, was parachuted into France by the SOE and did sterling work during the occupation. Badly wounded by the Germans while driving through Lot with André Malraux, he will often be referred to below.

The British military attaché came to see us again and launched into the same old spiel. It could be summed up in a single word – patience – but patience was precisely what we were running out of. Henri flatly informed him that we were withdrawing our promise not to escape and would endeavour to do so at the first opportunity.

One of our fellow internees was a very colourful personality named Jacques Pecheral, a journalist. He spoke fluent Spanish, which was a great help.

'I've got tooth trouble,' he told Henri. 'The camp MO sometimes sends dental patients to the hospital at Zaragoza. They leave in the morning and the guards escort them back to Jaraba at nightfall. I plan to leave but not return. I speak Spanish. I shall contrive to give the guards the slip at the hospital and take a taxi to Madrid. My problem is, I don't know where to go in Madrid. If you agree to give me a hand, I'll help you to escape and you can take me to the British embassy.'

Henri decided to try it. There was only one major problem: the MO. He lacerated his gums with a stick every morning for three or four days, then joined Pecheral outside the MO's office and reported sick. Their visit was a success. Three days later Henri and Pecheral were sent to the hospital in Zaragoza.

The guards escorted them to the hospital's casualty department and went for a stroll. Having submitted to the dentist's attentions, Henri and Pecheral calmly walked out of the hospital. Pecheral, in his fluent Spanish, hailed a taxi. Some hours later Henri was enjoying his first whisky and soda at the embassy in Madrid.

Before leaving camp Henri had been worried by the fact that his forthcoming venture would mean abandoning me there. He proposed that I should try to get away across the mountains and head for the Zaragoza-Madrid highway, where I was to wait for him at a place we had pinpointed on the map.

'I'll ask the taxi driver to wait ten minutes,' he said. It was a risky and uncertain arrangement. That said, we calculated that he would pass the prearranged spot between three and four o'clock in the afternoon. I invited my friend Jean-Claude to accompany me, and we left very early in the morning so as to reach the rendezvous ahead of time. Getting away was difficult, not because of the guards, who were still fast asleep, but because the rocky slopes around Jaraba were hard to climb. We trekked through the mountains for hours. Thanks to Jean-Claude, a tank commander and excellent navigator, we arrived at our rendezvous utterly exhausted but on time, that is to say, at three o'clock. We waited for a good hour, but no one showed up. Realizing that we would never get to Madrid this way, we retraced our steps to Jaraba, where, as luck would have it, our absence had gone unnoticed.

★   ★   ★

Henri Peulevé told me later on, in England, that he and Pecheral had halted the taxi at our rendezvous for five minutes but could wait no longer because the driver seemed suspicious of their odd behaviour. It was three o'clock when they drove on.

Some days after Henri's escape I was summoned to the office of the camp commandant, a colonel, who told me that I was leaving at once for Madrid. I hurried off to get ready and boarded a bus with twenty other prisoners.

What was afoot? I had no idea. At Madrid we were installed in a first-class hotel. Soon afterwards a British representative turned up and asked me to accompany him to his embassy. I was just preparing to leave when he took me aside.

'Before we go I'd like to introduce you to someone who's doing splendid work here for escapers from France. In view of her position, we must be discreet.' He indicated the door of an adjoining room. 'In there. She'll be delighted to see you.'

I followed him in, and was confronted out of the blue by a cousin of mine: Jacqueline, the daughter of my father's brother, who had married a very upper-crust Spaniard before the war. Count Benjuma by name, he was well regarded in Francoist circles. Jacqueline kissed me warmly.

'You can understand why I have to be careful. My husband has no idea of my activities.' She dabbed her eyes and added, 'I'm a Frenchwoman first and foremost.'

Having said goodbye to Jacqueline after far too brief a reunion, I accompanied the British representative to the embassy, where I was welcomed by the military attaché I had met at Jaraba. He shook my hand enthusiastically.

'You see?' he said. 'The Spaniards are becoming more cooperative. It's a good sign – we must be winning the war. In the meantime I've got some orders for you. You're to get to England as soon as possible. The Spaniards will be sending you in convoy to Algeciras. There you'll board a ship bound for England or North Africa, it doesn't matter which. You'll be picked up at sea and taken to Gibraltar. *En attendant*, old boy, let's have a brandy.'

I've never forgotten that Spanish brandy – in fact I even remember its name: 'Cognac Bertola'. I downed one glass, then

43

another, and got plastered for the first time in my life!

Everything went as the military attaché had foretold. After a wearisome but uneventful train journey from Madrid to Algeciras we refugees from France were put aboard a ship. Where was she bound for? We had no idea. She sailed slowly out of Algeciras harbour. A launch flying the British flag approached, two officers came up the side, and the public address system crackled into life.

'Lieutenant Poirier report to the bridge!'

It wasn't a very discreet summons.

I introduced myself.

'If you'll come with us, sir.'

The launch put me ashore a few minutes later. I was in Gibraltar.

Gibraltar

A fortress on a war footing, the Rock made a simultaneously formidable and peaceful impression. It had taken me almost six months to join our allies and come to rest beneath the flag of a country engaged in all-out war against the Nazis. It was a long journey, but those six months had helped me to mature in a singular way.

The dreamy, idealistic, rather quixotic young man who left Cannes had come of age. Just as certain African tribesmen prove their manhood by going off alone into the forest to kill a wild beast, so my odyssey had made a man of me. I felt resolute, judicious, sensible. I knew that by setting foot on Gibraltar's rocky shore I had plunged headlong into the war and was going to make my own contribution to the death of 'the beast'.

An officer escorted me to a handsome block of flats. There was a superb apartment on the second floor: a handsome sitting-room with a well-stocked bar, a gleaming bathroom, a comfortable bedroom.

'Make yourself at home,' the officer told me before leaving. 'Relax, get changed. I'll pick you up for dinner around seven-thirty.'

'Get changed . . .' I looked at myself in the mirror and burst out laughing. Six months ago I had left Cannes in an old shirt, a worn pair of slacks, a lumber-jacket, and a pair of suede shoes. I was still wearing the same old things, except that they had crossed the Pyrenees and shared my six months' captivity in the interim. Besides, I had lost some thirty pounds, so everything hung loose on me. The shoes had suffered worst of all. Mountains and suede shoes don't really mix.

Still chuckling, I had a delicious shower and got back into my old clothes. Just then there was a knock at the door and a soldier appeared.

'I'm your batman, sir. Anything I can do for you?' I was tempted to ask him to lend me his uniform but restrained myself. My British hosts would have considered it 'bad form', I felt sure.

The officer came to see how I was getting on. Looking at me, he suddenly grasped my predicament.

'I'm sorry,' he said, 'I should have taken you off to do a bit of shopping first. Don't worry, there's plenty of time. We'll drop in at the office. I'll draw you some money, and you can buy yourself a few things in Main Street before this evening.'

Having solemnly made me sign a receipt, he handed me a few pounds and accompanied me to the shops. I bought two shirts and a pair of slacks. I was going to invest in some new footwear as well, but I thought better of it. My old suede shoes had taken me this far, I reflected, so they'd earned the right to accompany me to England. They were museum pieces. At the risk of shocking His Britannic Majesty's representative, I decided to hang on to them.

Our next port of call was a military headquarters, where I was delighted to be greeted like a general. A colonel offered me a cigar and outlined my schedule.

'We've received detailed instructions about you. You're to get to London as soon as possible. Your plane leaves tomorrow. It will make an intermediate stop at Lisbon, where you'll spend part of the night. We're providing you with a British passport. If there's any problem, insist that you're a British subject. No one can relieve you of that passport except your outfit in England. An officer will meet your plane in London and take you on to SOE headquarters. Meanwhile, have a good time tonight and the best of luck.'

It was a balmy evening, and Royal Navy men on shore leave

were living it up in the bars along Main Street. Personally, I had to keep a clear head for tomorrow. After an excellent dinner in the mess I went back to my nice apartment like a good boy.

The next day two officers came to escort me to the airfield.

I presented myself at the check-out desk. My passport was examined and returned without comment. I was then directed to an aircraft in which I leisurely installed myself with my little travelling-bag tucked beneath my feet. It rather saddened me to be leaving Gib so soon – the Rock had been my first taste of freedom, after all – but I was also very excited to be on the verge of what I then regarded as a great adventure. My day-dream was interrupted by one of the officers who had accompanied me to the airfield. He bent down and whispered in my ear.

'We've got a minor problem,' he said. 'You're on our top priority list, but there's a general here who's most anxious to get to London by tonight. We can't do anything about it unless you volunteer to give up your seat as an act of simple courtesy. If you do, I promise to get you on the next plane out, i.e. within forty-eight hours.'

'Will you lend me the same apartment?' I asked.

He laughed and said, 'Of course.'

I retrieved my bag and got out. The general passed me without a glance and boarded the plane in my place. That night I decided to take greater advantage of what Gibraltar had to offer, so it was quite late by the time I got back to the apartment. I was just going to bed when the telephone rang. It was one of the officers I knew.

'You're a lucky devil,' he said. 'We'll be right over – tell you then.'

Minutes later three officers turned up looking very pale and solemn. I offered them a whisky. Then I asked what had happened.

'It's like this,' said one of them, even paler than the others. 'The plane you were meant to take this afternoon was shot down after leaving Lisbon. You're lucky to be alive.'

I took a big swallow of whisky.

'Cheers,' they said.

★　　★　　★

46

I learned later that one of the passengers in the plane the Germans shot down – under the impression that Winston Churchill was on board – was the celebrated British film actor Leslie Howard.

Everyone was shocked and saddened by this news, and the atmosphere during my last full day in Gibraltar was considerably more subdued. We took off the next afternoon and made an intermediate stop at Lisbon as scheduled. The plane was half empty, and the pilot came to have a word with me before we disembarked.

'You must have heard what happened to the last plane out of here,' he said. 'It's obvious that someone at the Lisbon end must have tipped off the Germans about its time of departure. This time we'll be doubly careful. We'll leave at night and keep our take-off time under wraps.'

I presented my passport to a member of the Portuguese immigration service, who examined it carefully before handing it back with a 'Thank you, sir, enjoy your stay.' I was startled. The man had addressed me in French!

We and the crew were then driven to a good Lisbon hotel.

I had time enough, during the few hours we spent there, to absorb the extraordinary atmosphere of the Portuguese capital in wartime. Seated on a café terrace, I heard people conversing in English, German, Italian, French, and – just occasionally – Portuguese. I felt I was dreaming, but then, Portugal was not at war.

It must have been one in the morning when someone knocked on my door. It was a member of the crew.

'We're leaving in ten minutes,' he said. 'Down to the lobby as quick as you can.'

We drove to the airport and took off forty minutes later. We flew without lights of any kind. It was dreary, sitting there in the dark, and I felt a trifle apprehensive, but I finally dozed off. I was awakened by some severe turbulence. Shortly afterwards the pilot came aft.

'We're an hour out from England,' he told us, 'but I'm sorry, the weather over London is so bad we've been diverted to Bristol.'

To me Bristol was as much England as London, so the news didn't really worry me.

We landed at Bristol under a grey, heavily overcast sky. Men in uniform were bustling around, and the general impression was one of brisk activity. We were in a land very much at war. I felt deeply moved as I set foot on the soil of a country which to me represented the last European bastion of liberty – one whose inhabitants' courage and fortitude had won the admiration of the entire free world.

I walked over to the little airport building, happy in the knowledge that whoever had been meeting me in London would have been notified by the authorities at Bristol, and that I would have no problems. I handed my British passport to an immigration officer, who asked me some questions. Remembering the instructions I had been given at Gibraltar, I solemnly explained, in my very Gallic English, that I was a British citizen but had spent part of my boyhood in France, hence my 'slight' French accent. The man seemed satisfied and returned my passport without a word. Thoroughly reassured, I made my way to a kind of waiting-room and was looking around for a reception committee when two officers walked up to me. One of them asked me to accompany them into a small office.

'Terribly sorry,' he said, 'but we'll have to check your story – there's a war on, you know. May I have your passport?'

I was faintly disconcerted, but I kept calm.

'Look,' I said, 'they're expecting me in London.'

'Who's "they"?' I was asked.

The situation was becoming complicated. For one thing, I didn't know who had been supposed to meet me in London; for another, the instructions I had been given in Gibraltar were quite explicit: I was to maintain that I was British and decline to surrender my passport to anyone but my superiors in the SOE – who were totally unknown to me.

'Very well,' said one of the officers.

He pressed a buzzer and two men in plain clothes entered.

'I'm handing you over to these gentlemen. They'll escort you to London.'

And that was how, within a few hours of my arrival in England, I found myself back in prison.

'Prison' is probably something of an exaggeration, but that was very much how I felt. After all I'd been through in the previous six months, just to get to England, I found it hard to reconcile

48

myself to the fact that my first night in the last remaining free country in Europe was to be spent in captivity.

In reality, I spent it in an establishment situated on the outskirts of London and curiously entitled the 'Patriotic School'. The authorities had transformed this property into a kind of concentration camp, and I soon discovered that all foreigners arriving in Britain without a plausible story were confined there until their identity and antecedents had been investigated. A large number of Frenchmen were sent to the 'Patriotic School'. Some spent only a short time there before going on to distinguish themselves in the Free French Forces; others, whose stories had failed to convince the British authorities, remained there longer. I quite understood why the British had to be so wary of foreigners arriving on their soil in wartime, even if they came as allies who were sincerely eager to join the armed forces. In my own particular case, however, I couldn't help wondering what my friend Henri Peulevé and his outfit were doing. Welcomed with open arms in Gibraltar, detained in London . . . I was starting to get annoyed.

The explanation, when I heard it a little later, was quite simple. Two SOE representatives had been waiting for me in London, sure enough, but no one ever informed them that my plane had landed at Bristol. The SOE took three days to find me, so it wasn't until my fourth day in custody that the camp commandant sent for me and handed me over to two SOE officers.

'Sorry about the foul-up,' said one of them. 'If you'll come with us, we'll take you to Orchard Court.'

IV
ENGLAND

Special Operations Executive

It is now time to present a brief account of this very special organisation.

The SOE [Special Operations Executive] dated from 1940, when the British High Command set it up at Churchill's request. Its principal task was to conduct subversive operations throughout occupied Europe. The French section was headed by Colonel Maurice Buckmaster.

Originally controlled by the Ministry of Economic Warfare, the SOE was later directly subordinated to Chief of Staff, Supreme Allied Command (COSSAC). Its functions were as follows:

(1) to assist in the recruitment of patriotic persons in enemy-occupied territory with a view to waging guerrilla warfare before and after the Allied landing, and, for the same purpose, to carry out air drops of arms and equipment over the said territories; and

(2) to plan and mount attacks and sabotage operations against enemy lines of communication for the purposes of D-Day, and to train specialist teams to carry out such missions.

On 6 May, 1941, Commandant [Major] Bégué was parachuted into France, the first officer to enter occupied France by that means. The French section of SOE subsequently landed another three hundred-plus officers by parachute. Some forty-five resistance networks were established and six hundred air drops carried out. The price of such an effort was heavy. Many SOE officers died in combat or in German custody. Generally speaking, the members of the SOE's French section were either British officers with a good knowledge of France or Frenchmen who had become intimately associated with the SOE's war effort in the course of resistance operations.

It may seem surprising, but at no time before crossing the threshold of Orchard Court had I imagined that I would be joining an essentially British organization. I was insufficiently aware of certain differences of opinion prevailing between General de Gaulle and the British authorities, nor had I any idea that the Free French had set up an organization of their own with a field of operations similar to that of the SOE. I was unsurprised that all the people I had met in Gibraltar and since my arrival in England were British, because it struck me as natural, if not desirable, that an organization operating from Britain should be primarily local in structure. I cannot say that it worried me to learn of the rivalry between the two services. I had come to fight a war, and that was what I did.

I am still proud of having belonged to an organization that not only played a vigorous and effective part in liberating my native land but proved capable of uniting the flower of French and British youth in a common cause. I have never felt that my service in the SOE was a form of disloyalty to General de Gaulle, for whom I always cherished the greatest respect, gratitude and admiration. On the contrary, I am convinced that I served my country, the Allies and the cause of freedom better in that efficient organization than I would have done in another, albeit equally courageous.

Orchard Court was the name of a luxury block of flats near Oxford Street, one floor of which was occupied by the offices of the French section of the SOE. I was accompanied there by one of the SOE officers who had rescued me from the 'Patriotic School'. He rang the bell and promptly withdrew. The door was answered by a man who ushered me inside with a friendly smile and asked my name.

'Poirier?' he said in French. 'Oh yes, please come this way.'

He showed me into a bathroom containing a magnificent black marble bidet. (This bathroom, which was familiar to every SOE agent, functioned as a waiting-room whenever our friend Park – the man who had greeted me – did not want us to be seen by other visitors to the French section.)

I waited between the bathtub and the bidet for a good ten minutes. Then the door opened and a delightful but enigmatic-looking girl invited me to join her in her office.

'I'm Vera Atkins,' she said. 'I think we should have a few minutes' chat. First of all, we've booked you a room at the Kensington Hotel in Knightsbridge. I think you'll be comfortable there. We also think, for security reasons, that you should change your name. I've got some papers for you made out in the name of Lieutenant Jack Peters. Will that suit you?' She didn't wait for an answer. 'Oh yes, and I'm going to give you a little advance on your pay. I'm sure you need it. I should also tell you that it isn't done to chat in the corridors. Our mentor, Park, knows his job. He'll make sure you never bump into anyone.' She smiled. 'Apart from staff, of course.'

The girl's flow of words had left me rather bemused. I felt intimidated by such a combination of good looks and efficiency. She jolted me out of my reverie by announcing that she was going to take me to see Colonel Buckmaster.

The colonel was a tall, lean man, very English but very affable. He got up from behind his desk and shook hands.

'How do you do, Jack, I've heard a lot about you. You've done some good work, but I trust you'll do some even better work from now on.' Where on earth was Henri, I wondered, but Buckmaster was speaking again. 'We've obtained you a lieutenant's commission in the army. We're just waiting for the papers to come through. Get yourself a uniform. In London, civilians of your age tend to be looked at askance. Well, Jack, delighted to welcome you aboard. First we plan to send you on a course and train you in all the aspects of our rather peculiar form of warfare. After that, we'll send you back into France. Henri has asked me to appoint you his second-in-command next time out. I'll think it over, but it seems a good idea, on the face of it.'

'Excuse me for asking,' I said, 'but where is Henri?'

'In this job one doesn't ask such questions. That course of yours will do you good.'

I was rather taken aback, but Buckmaster smilingly reassured me.

'Your friend Henri is away on a course in Scotland, but you'll see him in a day or two. Meantime, have a nice, quiet week in

London. Eat as well as you can, build up your strength, put on a bit of weight. Your training will be no picnic, believe me.' He rose, signifying that the interview was at end. 'See Bourne before you go.'

I left the colonel's office and hurried up to Park, the Cerberus of a doorman, whose expression turned wary as soon as he saw me.

'I want to see Bourne,' I told him.

'I suppose you mean Major Bourne Patterson,' he said tartly.

I made my way to the major's office, where he proceeded to ask me all kinds of questions about my studies, the towns I knew, my favourite sports, et cetera.

'The thing is,' he said, 'we're going to prepare a good cover story for your return to France. For that I'll need to become better acquainted with you, so I know what pieces to put into the jigsaw puzzle and what to leave out.'

I was a nice young Frenchman named Jacques Poirier when I entered Orchard Court. Two hours later I emerged as Jack Peters, a subaltern in the British army.

Back to School

Three days after my first visit to the offices of the SOE, when I was really beginning to find my way around London, I at last met up again with Henri Peulevé. He was in fine fettle, and told me all about his journey from Spain to England.

'The embassy people at Madrid weren't too pleased to see me at first. The military attaché fixed me up with some Spanish papers that said I was deaf and dumb, so I wasn't allowed to speak under any circumstances. I took the train to Algeciras, where our people picked me up and sneaked me aboard a ship bound for England. It was a frightful trip. We sailed in convoy, and the Germans attacked us again and again. Sometimes it was aircraft, often it was U-boats. A lot of ships were sunk. To cut a long story short, I only got here two weeks ago.'

It amused me to hear this, because in spite of Henri's colourful escape from Jaraba he had only just beaten me to England. He confirmed that he had asked if I could join him in France once my training was complete.

'It's an important mission in the south-west,' he said, 'but that's all I can tell you for the moment. First, you must get through your course successfully. Buckmaster and the others attach great importance to how agents behave in training.'

Then he changed the subject.

'What hotel did they put you in? I'll bet it's a lousy dump. Personally, I always stay at the Pastoria in Leicester Square. It's an amusing place, Churchill and Prince Bernhard of the Netherlands sometimes show up there. Buckmaster doesn't like us staying at the Pastoria, but who cares? Pick up your bag and I'll book you a room. We must have a bit of fun while you're here.'

Dear old Henri was a completely different person in London. To him it spelled total relaxation, and he soon introduced me to all the best nightspots in town. I was rather uneasy, though, because I didn't have much money. Henri merely scoffed at such petty considerations.

'I'll lend you some cash,' he told me. 'You can pay me back after the war.'

So I spent a week whooping it up as hard as anyone could in the middle of a war. After that Henri left to do a course in radio procedure and I received a summons from Orchard Court. It was goodbye to the Pastoria Hotel and off to my first training camp.

SOE officers assigned to carry out missions in enemy-occupied territory naturally had to undergo an intensive course of training designed to prepare them as fully as possible, both physically and in the techniques essential to their form of activity.

I was first sent to a training centre in the south of England. At this establishment, a school for commandos, we underwent a course of physical training and were taught to handle arms and explosives. Towards the end of the course, which lasted four weeks, we also attended classes in psychology, with the emphasis on interrogation by expert psychologists and psychiatrists. Some of their questions were so indelicate, I remember, that one day I told my interrogator, a colonel, to get lost. I regretted this after the event, being afraid that my reaction would affect my marks, but I heard no more of the incident.

After the Liberation I caught sight of the said colonel at an Allied military gathering in Paris. He recognized me at once, and told me in the course of conversation that he had given me an excellent mark because I had reacted precisely as a good SOE agent should.

The commando school was important to the SOE authorities because it enabled them to select and grade candidates undergoing training – or, of course, to reject them – at a relatively early stage.

I completed the course and was sent straight to a place near Mallaig in Inverness-shire, on the west coast of Scotland. I soon discovered that my previous course had indeed been a picnic by comparison.

The countryside was scenically superb but bleak and uninhabited. We were taught survival techniques and unarmed combat, the art of 'silent killing' and how to blow up railway tracks and trains – the saboteur's entire armoury, in other words. Navigation and map-reading were also included in the course, and I even learned how to drive a locomotive. The days and nights we devoted to mock attacks developed a spirit of comradeship and went a long way towards imparting a better perception of what was expected of us.

Some of our exercises were highly realistic. On one occasion, for example, we were ordered to attack a train on the Mallaig-Glasgow line. Leaving our base after dark, we trekked across country for three hours in very unpleasant conditions and reached the track not far from Mallaig. We were very keyed up, because the train was a normal passenger train, and we were not to let ourselves be spotted by regular army personnel.

We blackened our faces with a kind of soot and placed some maroons on the line. Then, concealed in the undergrowth, we waited for the train to appear. It emerged from the darkness with a long whistle, the maroons exploded, and it braked to a halt. We sprang to our feet and scrambled aboard, yelling and gesticulating. The passengers were ordinary, unsuspecting travellers, and I shall never forget the look on their faces when we burst in. I wonder how many of them thought the Germans had landed and how many realized that it was only a mock attack, albeit in rather bad taste, carried out by overexcited commandos. The operation lasted three minutes – just time enough to 'sabotage' the locomotive. Then we melted back into the darkness as quickly as we had boarded the train.

'Not bad,' was the verdict of the officer in charge of the exercise, 'but you rather overdid things.'

During this period I made an unexpected acquaintance. Among my father's friends was a very dynamic, talented businessman named Walter Watney, who had owned the Delage car company before the war. Resident in France when the Germans invaded, he and his family were in an awkward position and had to go to ground. My father did his best to help, and I had met Watney at my parents' place in Beaulieu a few days before setting off for England. Having gathered that I was about to leave, he surreptitiously slipped me his brother's address in London. 'Just in case,' he said with a smile. 'He's got a charming family. They'll help you and you can give them my news.'

My circumstances in England – the secrecy I had to observe and the fact that I had changed my name – naturally deterred me from getting in touch with people who knew my true identity, so I refrained from going to see Walter Watney's brother.

Some days after my arrival in Inverness-shire I got into conversation with one of my fellow trainees, a young British officer. After a few minutes he introduced himself.

'My name is Cyril Watney.'

I suppressed a start of surprise. 'Jack Peters,' I replied.

A week later, when we had just marched back through the mud after completing an arduous field exercise, Cyril came up to me.

'All this foot-slogging gets me down,' he said with a laugh. 'In France I'd be driving around in a nice big car.'

'I know,' I said. 'Your Uncle Walter would have lent you a Delage.'

It was Cyril's turn to be taken aback, so I told him my story. We became great friends, and I spent many weekends at the Watneys' London home when our course in Scotland ended. They completely adopted me, and I still cherish very fond memories of those who helped to provide me with a little of the warmth and affection I lacked so far from home.

Later on, by a coincidence no less surprising than that which had brought me into contact with the Watneys, I got to know another very hospitable family.

I returned to London for a few days after completing my course in Scotland. It had been decided that I was once more to serve under Henri Peulevé's orders, so I set about preparing for my next mission.

Wishing to familiarize myself with the area in south-west France where I was to be landed by parachute, I went to the Orchard Court library but searched in vain for the relevant map. I was just leaving when a young officer came in with a map in his hand — the one I'd been looking for. I was surprised because, notwithstanding all the SOE's security measures, I could hardly fail to infer that the young man was also planning a trip to the south-west. Catching sight of me, he apologized and introduced himself.

'George Hiller.'

'Jack Peters,' I said. (George Hiller, it will be remembered, was the youthful pacifist whose family knew mine, and whom Jean-Claude Servan-Schreiber had mentioned in the camp at Jaraba.)

George suggested that we have dinner together. In the course of the evening I jumped the Rubicon once more by revealing my real name and the connection between our respective families. George was delighted and invited me home the following Sunday.

'But you mustn't say anything about this outfit to my parents,' he told me. 'I've been careful not to tell my family what I do, least of all my mother. She thinks I'm a shirker, and it's better that way. She may get suspicious if you turn up with a different name, so you must be Jack Peters to her.'

And that was how I acquired another adoptive family in England. George's mother was a charming, very elegant Frenchwoman who always gave me a cordial welcome, but she was ignorant of my true identity throughout my time in London.

Major George Hiller was parachuted into the south-west of France, and Cyril Watney became his radio operator. In 1944 George was ambushed by the Germans while travelling in a car with André Malraux. Though badly wounded, he managed to escape, and the RAF performed a minor miracle by picking him up from Lot in a light aircraft. It wasn't until he was safely in an

English hospital that he told his mother about the magnificent work he had been doing and, at the same time, disclosed my identity.

To revert to my spell of training in Scotland, it was arduous as well as extremely interesting. However, the spirit of comradeship that grew up between us all provided certain compensations.

The camp commandant was a red-faced Scot, very strict when necessary but full of humour when off duty. He enjoyed relaxing in our company, and, like all good Scotsmen, considered whisky an essential accompaniment to any festivity. Whisky was in short supply, however, because the inhabitants of Mallaig disliked relinquishing their national beverage to outsiders, especially Sassenachs. The commandant, good psychologist that he was, devised a plan. One day he summoned me into the middle of the school courtyard and called my fellow trainees to attention. He returned my salute, removed my badges of rank, and addressed me crisply.

'I've an important mission for you, Peters: you're to go to Mallaig and find us some whisky. Good luck.'

I duly set off for Mallaig in the school's small motor launch. Having combed every pub, bar, and drinking den in Mallaig, I returned with two whole cases of whisky. Everyone was drawn up on parade when I got back with my booty. There was a repetition of the ceremony that had attended my departure, except that this time my badges of rank were returned by a beaming major. I had to repeat this operation two or three times while in Scotland.

Within a few weeks, my course in Scotland had turned me into an explosives expert and a specialist in close combat. I had finally graduated from Britain's strangest 'university'.

In good physical shape, I spent a few days in London before being sent to Ringway, a parachute school near Manchester. I shall refrain from describing all the techniques they drummed into us before we were actually dropped from an aircraft. Suffice it to say that I found the ordeals we underwent on the ground infinitely more difficult and dangerous than the real thing. Finally, I made my first jump. I must have thought my parachute would never open. When it did, I was so ecstatic that I started shouting and waving my arms like a madman. I was brusquely called to order at the last moment by a sergeant armed with a loud-hailer.

'Keep your legs together, you bloody fool!'

I made some other, more successful jumps. Then, after another brief stay in London, I was sent to yet another, very peculiar training establishment.

This school was situated in a manor house near Beaulieu, in the south of the New Forest. There was no more physical or paramilitary training. In the main, we were taught clandestine security techniques (behavioural studies, in modern parlance): how to react under interrogation, how to disguise one's own personality. It was far from easy, because our instructors took their job very seriously. They would sometimes dress up as Germans and give us a highly realistic idea of what we could expect if we were caught. In fact, while at the school we tried to live as we would have to live in enemy-occupied territory.

After some weeks I received instructions to go to Sheffield and play the secret agent there. I was given a list of self-styled fellow agents, some of them traitors, others friends. My task was to construct an espionage organization out of this mixed bag and report my progress to the school every day.

It took me only a few days to set up a network. I had, in fact, decided to distrust all the contacts given me by the school, and to work with people other than those on my list. Being unable to 'infiltrate' my burgeoning organization, the school authorities were left with no choice but to have me arrested by the Sheffield police. I had, however, come through with flying colours.

Opinions on the value of our training differed widely. I myself considered it good, but felt that more account should be taken of the fact that, once we were in France, things could turn out to be entirely different. A young agent should be made to realize that our training could convey only a sketchy idea of certain conditions that might develop in the field, and that it would be dangerous for us to regard it as a 'bible' for all occasions. Having already acquired some experience of clandestine activities in France, I had confidence in myself. Thanks to my toughening-up course in Scotland and my knowledge of certain techniques acquired at Beaulieu, I could hardly wait to get back to France and go into action.

After completing my training I caught a brief glimpse of Henri Peulevé, who was on the point of departure. His return was a tricky business. The injury he had sustained on his first mission precluded the use of a parachute, so the SOE had decided to send him back by plane. Henri flew to western central France in a Lysander, one of the light aircraft much favoured for such operations because of its ability to land and take off in a very small space. Just before leaving he sent me a note asking me to join him as soon as possible.

I have to confess that life in London had lost some of its appeal after the excitement of the training camps. I would idle away the mornings in town, then head for Orchard Court to study maps and papers or try to extract a few pounds from Vera Atkins. We were not exempt from financial problems, our meagre pay being the same as that of regular army officers of the same rank. Thanks to Vera, however, we were able to obtain advances on our pay, and I myself was almost ten months overdrawn by the time I left England. The result was that, when I returned there after the Liberation, I found that the sum due to me, after repayments, was just enough to buy me a decent dinner!

In the evenings I would quietly make my way back to the Pastoria Hotel. I spent a good deal of time with George Wilkinson, a very likeable fellow who had trained with me and had decided to stay there too. George, whose brother also belonged to the SOE, was a congenial companion. Sadly, he was arrested by the Germans when parachuted into France and died in a concentration camp.

One evening, while strolling in Piccadilly, George and I decided to have a drink in the bar at Oddenino's. An attractive young woman sat down at the next table, and we soon got talking to her. An hour later we were dining together à trois. Although she asked a lot of questions about what we were doing, we didn't attach much importance to the fact. Fresh from our training, we were adept at giving evasive replies and easily contrived to steer conversation into less perilous waters. In the end she invited us to have a nightcap at her hotel, the Dorchester.

It was a most enjoyable evening, but at Orchard Court two days later, when I was idly browsing through one of the German magazines which the SOE obtained by devious means from occupied Europe, something caught my eye. It was a photograph of a group of German officers with a young woman in their midst, laughing.

I studied the picture more closely. No doubt about it: she was the girl from the Dorchester. I consulted George, who was dumbfounded and confirmed my own impression. We went to see Bourne Patterson and informed him of our discovery. He, in turn, notified an officer in MI5, who asked us a number of questions. Some weeks later Bourne Patterson summoned me to his office.

'I just had a call from that chap in MI5,' he said tersely. 'He says to thank you both. Good work.'

When I turned up at Orchard Court a few days later, Park motioned me to follow him. 'The tailor's waiting for you,' was all he said.

He showed me into an office where a man in civilian clothes proceeded to take my measurements without a word. Finally he said, 'I've got to run you up two ultra-French outfits in double-quick time.'

Another man came in and made me try on various shirts and shoes, all ostensibly of French manufacture.

The inference was obvious: I would soon be off.

V
RETURN TO FRANCE

Henri Peulevé and Operation 'Author'

The Resistance and the SOE began their activities in France in 1941, and their first joint operation took place on 10 October, when men and arms were landed by parachute not far from Bergerac in the Dordogne.

I asked my friend Jean Le Harivel, a former SOE officer who took part in this preliminary operation (a monument commemorating it has since been erected near Villamblard), to describe how it went.

'Our parachute drop wasn't a great success,' Jean recalled with a smile. 'There were four of us: Hayes, Jumeau, Tuberville and I. For a start, three of us wound up in the trees around the drop zone and the fourth, Tuberville, came down quite a long way off. If the object had been to ensure that the containers didn't land on the parachutists' heads, it was amply fulfilled: they came down several kilometres from the drop zone.' Jean went on, 'But you ought to look up the account of the operation given by Albert Rigoulet, nicknamed *"Le Frisé"* ["Curly"], who was in charge on the ground. It appeared in the magazine section of *France-Soir* on 17 October 1981, forty years after the event.' Here is the gist of Rigoulet's account:

'In February, 1941, Georges Bégué (radio operator and instructor) had landed "blind" by parachute near Châteauroux. Through Pierre-Bloch (an anti-Pétainist deputy who had gone to ground at Villamblard), Max Hymans (later president of Air France), and Dr Dupuy (mayor of Villamblard), he established contact with Rigoulet, a local man whose father owned a farm at Bellacaud. He found an excellent landing ground which the SOE approved by getting the BBC to transmit the following message: *"Gabriel envoie ses amitiés"* [Gabriel sends his regards], On 2 October the BBC announced that *"Gabriel va bien"* [Gabriel is fine], but nothing happened. No aircraft overflew the landing ground.

'The message *"Gabriel va bien"* was not repeated until 10 October. Unhappily, the operation got off to a bad start. The plane arrived too soon and circled noisily at low altitude. The moonlight was brilliant, the reception committee had not yet turned up, and every dog in the district barked like mad. Having failed to see the prearranged signal lights, the plane flew off. It returned, as noisily as ever, and four men jumped. Three of them – Hayes and Jumeau (instructors assigned to set up networks) and Le Harivel (instructor and radio operator) – came down in the trees. The containers fell further away. The fourth man – Tuberville – landed solo and was arrested by gendarmes next day. Initially sent to the prison at Périgueux, he escaped by jumping from the train that was transporting him to another prison.

'In view of the previous night's racket, Rigoulet decided to hide the three parachutists at his father's farm instead of taking them into Bergerac. On leaving there a week later, they almost immediately fell into a trap at the Villa du Bois in Marseilles. In addition to the three parachutists, the authorities' haul included Pierre-Bloch, Raymond Roche (who had been landed on the Mediterranean coast by submarine), Robert Lyon (a friend of Pierre-Bloch's), and, worst of all, George Bégué, invaluable as an organizer and radio operator. Also arrested were Fleuret (letterbox), Garel, Trotobas, Liewer and Langelaan.

'They were all taken to the prison at Périgueux. As luck would have it, however, they were later transferred to the detention camp at Mauzac, whence all twelve of them escaped in July, 1942. With the active assistance of Gaby, Pierre-Bloch's wife, and the connivance of their guards, they got away by crawling under the barbed wire – an unoriginal but effective mode of procedure.

'Rigoulet took them under his wing once more, this time by picking them up in a van and driving them to a farm fifty kilometres from the camp. They lay low there for a week while false papers were procured for them. Then, travelling in twos and threes, they headed for Perpignan and Spain by way of Lyons. This operation was a success. They all got to England, though some of them spent time in Spanish prisons and the camp at Miranda del Ebro, which had a sinister reputation.

'Bégué later became head of radio communications at the SOE centre in England. Hayes, parachuted into Normandy, sent back some very valuable information prior to the landings. Robert Lyon, Liewer and Trotobas headed networks of their own. Jumeau, who was less fortunate, died in a concentration camp. Rigoulet continued to serve the Resistance by organizing air-drops and in 1943 helped to establish the Resistance cells that developed into the maquis units of the Dordogne.

'Jean Le Harivel, alias Philippe, became a leading organizer of air drops into occupied France at SOE headquarters in England.'

Although the operation on 10 October, 1941, was not a great success in itself, it bore fruit later on, initially in Dordogne and subsequently throughout occupied France.

On his first mission to France in the spring of 1942, Henri Peulevé had landed by parachute with Claude de Baissac, the intrepid Mauritian who headed his network. They jumped near Nîmes, but their plane was flying too low. Henri sustained a compound fracture of the leg on landing, as I have already mentioned, and was virtually disabled.

De Baissac, who set to work with a will, took less than a year to set up a powerful organization. Rendered vulnerable by its sheer size, however, it was later betrayed by André Grand-Clément, an air force officer, and almost completely destroyed. Thus, Henri Peulevé's instructions on his second mission to France were to establish a network in Corrèze and Dordogne, train specialist teams capable of attacking and sabotaging enemy lines of communication, and arrange air drops of arms and equipment for the Resistance organizations as a whole. He was also to seek contact with the new maquis units that were taking shape in the area, both FTP (the communist Franc-Tireurs et Partisans) and AS (Armée Secrète).

The 'Author' network commanded by Henri, alias Jean, grew rapidly and developed within a few months into a compact, efficient organization. He managed to get on good terms with the Dordogne FTP (no easy matter) and in particular, notably towards the end of 1943, with its new departmental chief, André Bonnetot, alias Vincent. The latter, who had come from the Paris region, quickly realized that it was in his maquis units' interest to establish good relations with the 'Author' network, this being the only means of obtaining the arms they so badly needed at the end of 1943. Vincent's position was a very responsible one. I later got to know him well and respect him highly. Henri arranged a few preliminary air drops and organized the arrival in Lot of George Hiller and Cyril Watney. George, code-named Maxime, set up an effective network entitled 'Footman'. Then Henri sent for me.

The Real Thing at Last

I was back in France, but under difficult circumstances. A Frenchman in England, I had just been christened an Englishman in France.

My young companion looked at me inquiringly. I briefly intimated that our strange reception committee did not fill me with confidence, and that it would be better for us to move on as soon as possible. Meantime, the members of the reception committee were busy appropriating our parachutes, doubtless intending to turn them into shirts. I interrupted their activities.

'We want to leave for Brive right away.'

'You can catch a through train to Brive from Marcillac in three hours' time.'

I asked to look at a map and discovered that our brilliant pilot, who should have dropped us two kilometres from Montignac in the Dordogne, had done so five kilometres from Marcillac-la-Croisille, a navigational error of some hundred kilometres.

I wasn't unduly worried, because London had allowed for a mistake of this kind. If I found no reception committee on landing, I was to make my way to Brive and knock on the door of the Bloc Gazo company in Avenue de la Gare. The local team calmed down a bit and invited us to have a snack and relax at a secluded cottage several kilometres away, where the Germans wouldn't find us. I agreed, albeit without enthusiasm, and we waited there patiently until it was time to leave for the station.

Was I tired or simply absent-minded? Whichever, I made my first mistake at the station. I walked up to the guichet and said, in English, 'A single to Brive, please.'

'*Que dites-vous?*' demanded the woman behind the window. I quickly pulled myself together.

'*Un billet pour Brive, s'il vous plaît, madame.*'

And to think I'd just spent nearly six months learning the tradecraft of a secret agent!

The train pulled into the station. I got in and sat down facing my companion, who was beginning to show dangerous signs of nerves. The train was full of field-grey uniforms, and there were two German officers in our compartment.

'A lot of them around this year,' I said, smiling across at my fellow agent.

I decided that the best way to avoid trouble would be to feign sleep, but my plan miscarried. I really did fall asleep and awoke with a start to find my companion deep in conversation with a farmer. Watched with interest by the two German officers, he was discoursing on the patriotic French author Charles Péguy.

The train pulled into Brive at last. My heart missed a beat when we got out – travellers were being scrutinized at the exit by a dozen German soldiers – but I squared my shoulders and walked firmly past them. Although we found the Avenue de la Gare without difficulty, Bloc Gazo was shut: a little notice on the door clearly stated that the business did not open on Sundays. Our situation was going from bad to worse. We at first considered checking into a hotel, but I thought better of it.

'Look,' I said, 'hotels are closely watched, and our papers may be dicey. We won't know if they're satisfactory until we've made contact with the Resistance.'

Talking as we went, we found ourselves outside Saint-Cernin Church and went in. We attended one Mass, then another – in fact I've never attended so many Masses in such a short space of time. Being unable to avail ourselves of the church's hospitality any longer, we went for a walk on a hill outside the town. Although it was early January, 1944, and very cold, we decided to spend the night in the open.

The next morning, chilled to the bone, we made our way back to Brive and Bloc Gazo. Henri was standing outside. He stared at me incredulously.

'What on earth are you doing here?'

'Don't ask me, ask the RAF,' I retorted. 'They really screwed us up. The stupid clots dropped us a hundred kilometres from Montignac.'

'I just don't understand it,' Henri said. 'I was at the landing ground at Montignac. The plane circled a couple of times and then flew off. I honestly thought you'd gone back to London.'

He dealt with my companion, who was urgently awaited by a network in the Poitiers area. Then, contentedly, he told me, 'Come along and I'll introduce you to my friends.'

The 'Author' Network

At Brive Henri had built up a very determined team whose headquarters were situated in the offices of the firm mentioned above, Bloc Gazo. This was owned by a Corrézien named Maurice Arnouilh, who was absolutely devoted to Henri and served the Resistance with distinction. Although slightly scatty and lacking in caution, Arnouilh was a most endearing character.

Henri had also recruited a very efficient *résistant* named Charles Delsanti, the former police chief of Ussel. Delsanti's police contacts and local knowledge made him an outstanding associate.

Henri received invaluable assistance from a very courageous couple named Paul and Georgette Lachaud of Daglan, near Domme in the Dordogne. Paul, alias Poulou, had placed his farmhouse at our disposal, and at one stage it housed a sizeable cache of arms.

Being not only extremely busy but having to act as his own radio operator, Henri was hard put to it to maintain contact with London in addition to all his other duties. Some days after I arrived Delsanti recommended him an excellent radio operator in the person of Louis Bertheau. Louis was a charming, shy young man who had been a radio operator in the French air force. He enthusiastically agreed to serve the network in that capacity and Arnouilh offered him a hide-out in a house on the road to Tulle occupied by one of his employees and his wife, Monsieur and Madame Lamorie.

Henri had taken only a few months to build up his network, as I have already said. He was forging closer links with the regional maquis and the first air drops were arriving. Henri also wanted to recruit a small combat unit capable of carrying out acts of sabotage and launching surprise attacks on the enemy, in compliance with precise instructions from the SOE, as soon as that type of swift and effective operation became necessary. The formation of this group was destined to accelerate a few days after my arrival.

In the course of my first evening at Brive, Henri told me about an extremely important meeting he had had, early in September, 1943, with someone whose support might count for a great deal. It was André Malraux.

'I have to admit I'm at a loss,' he confessed, 'because Malraux is absolutely determined to help us and play an active part. Under present circumstances, however, I feel that his personality and reputation may prove a major liability. He'll be recognized, and the Gestapo will do the rest. D-Day – that's when Malraux will be essential to the Liberation movement, not before. Anyway, you must meet him. He's a source of extremely valuable advice, you'll see.'

It was during my first encounter with Malraux that he recommended two potential recruits. The first was Raymond Maréchal.

'We were comrades in the Spanish Civil War. He's a bit of a desperado, a bit of an anarchist, but you need men of his type.'

Henri, who leapt at the idea, had found the ideal person to form his combat unit.

Malraux's second recommendation was altogether different from the first. It was his brother Roland.

Lunch with André Malraux

Some days after my arrival in Brive Henri told me that he had arranged to have lunch with Malraux at a small inn just outside town.

'You're coming with me,' he said, and added, 'George Hiller will be there too.'

Shall I be honest? I was more enthusiastic at the prospect of seeing my friend George than of making the acquaintance

73

of a famous author. I was curious, naturally, and recognized Malraux's importance to the needle match we would have to play until France was liberated, but I was only twenty-one years old. The only Malraux opus I knew was *La Condition Humaine*, and I was so preoccupied with making a success of my mission that the thought of meeting a literary lion did not excite me overmuch.

We drove to the restaurant in one of Arnouilh's gas-burning cars. I caught sight of George standing outside, and Henri, realizing how glad I was to see him again, tactfully went on ahead.

'I'll go and check on our guest,' he told me. 'Meantime, have a chat with your friend.'

George Hiller was in great form, but I soon discovered that to him this meeting with Malraux was a momentous occasion.

'Just imagine,' he said in awed tones, 'Malraux here!' And he went on to speak of his books, his career, his role in the Spanish Civil War.

I could tell that George, who was a few years older than I, really knew his Malraux. Those five minutes taught me more about the man I was to meet than I had gleaned in the whole course of my young life.

Then in his forty-second year, André Malraux was a native of Paris. His mother was half Italian, half of Jura stock, his father, Fernand Malraux, was an adventurous type – excessively so, perhaps, because his wife left him when André was four, taking the boy with her. André was, however, allowed to pay weekly visits to his father, who had remarried and given him two half-brothers, Roland and Claude, born in 1912 and 1920 respectively.

From his earliest days André was a great reader and a diligent pupil with a universal thirst for knowledge and understanding. He was also a great frequenter of museums, especially the Musée Guimet, whose exhibits stimulated his early fascination with the East. The magazine *La Connaissance* published his first article, '*Les origines de la poésie cubiste*', when he was eighteen.

In 1921 he married and set out on his travels. His first ports of call were Germany, Greece, Italy, Czechoslovakia and Spain. Then came the East: Angkor and the temple of Bantaí Srey, from which he detached some carved stones – an act that got him into serious trouble with the law but earned him considerable notoriety. It also bred an abhorrence of government-supported colonial exploitation and a sense of solidarity with the oppressed.

Back in France once more, he published *La Tentative de l'Occident* and was employed by Gallimard to supervise their artistic ventures. In 1929 he published *Les Conquérants* [*The Conquerors*], which won him the Inter-Allied Prize and a wide readership. This was followed by *La Voie Royale* [*The Royal Way*] and *La Condition Humaine* [*Man's Fate*], for which he was awarded the Prix Goncourt in 1933. The latter work, which established Malraux's literary stature once and for all, coincided with the rise of Nazism in Germany.

In 1936 came the Francoist insurrection. The then minister of aviation asked Malraux to go to Spain and find out how best to aid the Republicans. France resolved on a policy of non-intervention, but Malraux remained in Spain. He took part in the civil war, and it was largely thanks to him that the Spanish Republic formed an air force.

In 1937 he published *L'Espoir* [*Days of Hope*], a work that preceded the end of the war in Spain and the beginning of the war in France. The Republicans gave up, the fascists triumphed, Mussolini marched into Addis Ababa and Hitler into Vienna. Not many people shared the 'hope' of Malraux's title. It was Gide, however, who wrote that 'While so many others strive to disparage humanity, Malraux spontaneously exalts it.'

Such, in a nutshell, was the person I was about to meet.

We entered the restaurant. Our table was in a secluded position, probably by arrangement with Arnouilh, who had ordered the meal. I caught sight of Henri, then a man with his back to us. Henri simply said, 'May I introduce George and Jacques?'

Looking at André Malraux, I saw a runny eye, a snuffly nose, a face in perpetual motion. So much for my first impression of him.

Malraux stopped talking just long enough to shake hands, then resumed his monologue. I found it very hard to catch the drift. After one or two attempts, I discovered that – in between making numerous parenthetical allusions to Chinese art, the siege of Stalingrad, and Braque's technique – Malraux was analysing Lawrence of Arabia's military campaigns. I was not only dazzled and captivated but extremely perturbed. I remembered what Henri had said on my first night in Brive. With an associate like this, we would be detected and picked up by the Gestapo before a week was out.

In a more relaxed mood towards the end of the meal, Malraux chatted to us very pleasantly about his brother Roland, Raymond Maréchal, and his dealings in Paris with the CNR (*Comité national de la Résistance*).

I never dreamed then that events would forge a close association between me and Malraux, who became – to our mutual advantage, I believe – my daily companion in the months that followed.

The 'Author' Network, continued

Henri had no real wish to specify my duties, preferring me to keep abreast of all the network's activities. The result was that we very often went on missions together.

Some days after my arrival I had to call at the Lachauds' farm to make arrangements for an air drop, so I got to know Poulou and Georgette. We could count without question on their courage, dedication and loyalty, and Henri had indeed been fortunate to find them.

The BBC broadcast the message announcing the air drop on the night I arrived. Poulou had discovered a suitable landing ground near Domme, so we went there and waited. I checked that the beacons were in place and paced up and down to keep the biting cold at bay. At five a.m. we had to face the fact that the plane wasn't coming. We spent the next night in the open as well, by which time I was starting to feel ill and couldn't stop shivering. Still the plane didn't come. Finally, on the third day, the message was repeated. Barely able to stand after two nights without sleep, I accompanied Poulou to the landing ground once more.

Towards eleven p.m. we distinctly heard the sound of aircraft engines. I flashed the prearranged signal with my torch and the plane flew right overhead, dropping fifteen containers as it went. Poulou and his little team collected our precious haul and loaded it into an old truck. By the time we got back to the farm I was really ill and running a temperature of 104-plus. Georgette ordered me to bed.

'He'll have to be cupped,' she decreed.

I was aghast, never having been subjected to such treatment, but Georgette ignored my reaction. With the help of her friends Solange and Lucienne she turned me this way and that, applying the horrible cups to my back and chest in turn. I went to sleep for thirty-six hours. When I finally awoke, I was better.

I often had dealings with Vincent Bonnetot, the FTP's regional commander. He was a man of courage and discretion, and I was happy to work with him. We had to select several landing sites together. It wasn't too easy to get around at this period, because Dordogne and Corrèze were under close surveillance and we often ran into road-blocks manned by Germans or Vichy militiamen. Thanks to the good offices of Maurice Arnouilh my identity card was genuine, having been issued by the town hall at Brive. I had become Jacques Perrier, timber merchant, one of Arnouilh's employees and a large-scale purchaser of wood for his gas generators. That said, every road-block was an ordeal. The Germans would have done better to check our pulse-rate than our papers!

One afternoon I had arranged to meet Vincent at Brive and survey a landing ground in the north of Corrèze. Maurice Arnouilh was to accompany us in his own car, a Chevrolet officially converted to run on gas, though he could, by pressing a button, switch to petrol if we needed to go fast. We were not always armed, but that day Vincent and I had brought a Sten gun with us and hidden it under the seat in case of accidents.

We came to a road-block, where our papers were closely examined. Maurice, all smiles, did his best to charm the Germans. At last, without asking us to get out of the car, the officer in charge waved us on.

I met Raymond Maréchal, Malraux's recommended candidate, at Poulou's farm. A formidable-looking man, he had been so badly wounded during the Spanish Civil War that a surgeon had inserted a steel plate in his forehead. Although this distorted his face a good deal and lent him a ferocious air, he proved to

77

be a very likeable character. Raymond was indeed a desperado, as Malraux had told us, but he was also a force of nature, and as brave as he was astute. He had already rescued several of his comrades and did not join us empty-handed. He immediately grasped what we expected of him and set to work without delay.

I had taken a room in the same hotel as Henri, the Hôtel Champanatier not far from Brive station, but once the Lamories' house became an operational base for our radio transmissions I had to go and live there. I was not exactly overjoyed by my new residence because it presented certain dangers. The Lamorie family lived on the ground floor and we occupied the floor above. It was a very unpretentious establishment – just one room whose only access was a narrow staircase. The furniture consisted of a bed and a table with our radio transmitter on it. There was also a wardrobe in which Henri had stowed some weapons and explosives (the plastic explosives that were then coming into general use).

I would happily have put up with these quarters if I had not received so many visits there from our friends. Members of the network were beginning to haunt the house with undue frequency. I told Henri what I thought.

'Our security needs tightening up, and quickly,' I said. 'There are too many comings and goings. Some members of the network are getting careless. We ought to be more cautious.'

Henri's initial response was to explain that there were two types of operation, one based on caution, the other on risk-taking.

'The first type will get us nowhere. The second could get us caught, but it's the only road to success.'

Although I didn't disagree with him, I thought that a more satisfactory arrangement should be feasible. Henri readily agreed, and we decided to consult the entire team on the possibility of finding another house for our radio transmissions.

'Meanwhile,' said Henri, 'I'd like you to move back into the Champanatier.'

Our work was becoming increasingly risky. Henri had originally found it difficult to establish contact with the leading lights of the Resistance. Now that we were becoming known, certain maquis commanders tried to contact us direct.

Leaks were always possible, and we had to be more and more careful of the contacts we maintained. At the same time, it was our job to remain constantly on the move, either to reconnoitre landing grounds or to locate arms dumps and meet with Resistance leaders. We also had to remain in close touch with Raymond Maréchal, who was actively recruiting a combat unit capable of going into action as soon as the Allies gave the word.

During 1941 and 1942 most Resistance activists had belonged to movements or networks inspired by General de Gaulle or by patriotic individuals based in France. They ran considerable risks, few in number though they were, because they were threatened not only by the Germans but by French informers and the Vichy police. Many of them were arrested and their networks destroyed. These were the men who laid the foundations of the Resistance, which developed along different lines from 1943 onwards. The small groups that took shape in rural areas grew and multiplied in the course of that year. This was the start of the maquis.

A district commander of the FFI *(Forces Françaises de l'Interieur)* was appointed to every district in which the maquis were developing (the bulk of our own sphere of operations came under District R5). These district commanders encountered numerous problems because they had, in principle, to wield authority over two entirely disparate and often rival organizations: the AS *(Armée Secrète)* and the communist FTP *(Francs-Tireurs Partisans)*. Their task was made even harder by the distances they had to travel, which rendered communication between them and the maquis quite hazardous.

The maquis commanders, many of whom had founded their own units, were very independent individuals. This being so, it was pretty clear that Henri and I would have to establish a sound working relationship with them without, of course, short-circuiting the FFI's chain of command.

As the Resistance grew, so we had to augment our little group. One welcome addition was Roland Malraux, whom André introduced to us in person. Roland was altogether different from his half-brother. Dapper and rather sophisticated but extremely likeable, he impressed us as someone who would fit in very quickly. He joined us early in March, 1944.

We acquired another recruit at the same period, one whose appearance in our midst was a source of astonishment to me.

Some days before Roland Malraux arrived, Henri told me that he had received a message warning him to expect a visit from a *résistant* from Savoie whose cover had been blown there, and who might possibly be useful to us. A password had been agreed, and Henri, who had to visit some maquis units in the Dordogne, asked me to interview the said Savoyard and decide whether we could use him.

A meeting was arranged. I was a trifle wary and regretted that Bloc Gazo itself should have been selected as the rendezvous. We had a hiding-place under the company's offices, a cellar to which we gained access by way of a trapdoor and a ladder. Having decided to receive our visitor in this bolt-hole, I settled myself behind a desk with my revolver secreted in a half-open drawer, just in case.

After a few minutes a member of the network left on watch upstairs came to tell me that the newcomer had arrived and knew the password perfectly. I said to send him down. The first I saw of him through the open trapdoor was a pair of shoes and his trouser-legs. The man carefully descended the ladder with his back to me, reached the ground, and turned. It was my father! I was flabbergasted. Our eyes met, and he got the message at once.

'*Bonjour, monsieur*,' I said quickly. Then, to the lookout who was following him down, 'It's all right, thanks. You can go back upstairs and shut the trapdoor.' A moment later my father and I were delightedly hugging each other.

My father's arrival presented me with a problem. I was eager for him to join us, knowing that his sang-froid and resourcefulness would be a major asset to the network, but absolutely determined that no one should know of our relationship (except Henri, who knew him from Beaulieu). Everyone thought I was English, and it would have seemed rather odd for an Englishman parachuted into France to have a father who didn't speak a word of Shakespeare's native tongue.

But I had another reason for hesitation. I would have to be, and intended to be, his boss. Would he accept that? I explained my misgivings, and he agreed that we both had a problem.

'I suggest we meet again tomorrow,' he said. 'Let's sleep on it.'

The next morning I had another meeting with my father – 'Commandant [Major] Robert', as he became known in the Resistance. We had arranged to meet in the restaurant of our hotel. He came towards me with a broad smile.

'À vos ordres, Capitaine,' was all he said.

'Commandant Robert' could not come to us right away because he had one or two problems to sort out, so we agreed that he should join us in two or three weeks' time.

Henri, back from visiting his maquis units, was quite as surprised to see my father as I had been. We told him of our plan over lunch, and he promptly approved.

'As long as no one spots the resemblance,' he said, 'I'm sure it would be much the best thing.'

My father gave me news of my mother. Then, noticing how tired Henri was looking, he suggested that he go and stay with her for a few days.

'It would do you good. You can give her news of Jacques. He can go and see her too, later on, but not right away. Imagine if he knocked on the door without warning – it would be too much of a shock!'

Henri pronounced this a good idea, and my father departed.

Disaster Strikes

Henri had intended to leave for Savoie on 20 March or thereabouts, but he was still there on the evening of that day. He came over to me.

'You know,' he said, 'that was a silly idea of your father's. You're itching to see your mother again and she can't wait to see you, but I'm the one who's going. It's absolute nonsense. You must leave for Savoie tomorrow.'

I protested. I argued that he needed the rest and that we had all agreed on the trip, but he wouldn't hear of it.

'I'm the boss, and you're going,' he told me. 'That's an order. Just be back in four or five days.'

I retired to my room, packed my little travelling-bag, and went to bed. At seven the next morning, while I was shaving, Henri put his head round the door.

'Have a good trip, old boy. Give Kiou a big hug from me,' he said, and shut the door again. (I had nicknamed my mother 'Kiou' some years before. I can't remember why.)

I walked to the station, quite oblivious of the potential dangers of the trip and feeling more like a soldier on leave.

Two hours after I left, Henri was at the Lamories' house with Bertheau, who was getting in touch with London by radio. Delsanti and Roland Malraux were seated at the table, chatting quietly.

Maurice Arnouilh, late as usual, quickened his step. He was just about to cross the Tulle-Brive road, only a hundred metres short of the Lamories' house, when his heart missed a beat: two black Citroën saloons were parked outside. At that moment the door opened and out they filed one by one, those friends whose ordeal had only just begun, escorted by Germans armed with submachine-guns.

Maurice turned on his heel. Hurrying back to his car, which was parked outside his house, he drove to the Verlhacs' at Quatre-Routes.

'We must warn Jacques,' he told them.

A few hours later Georgette came down to Brive from the Moulin du Couzoul to deliver some air-drop details for transmission to London. She fell into a German trap and was arrested. With remarkable presence of mind, she managed to swallow the tell-tale papers and was eventually released, thereby preserving us all from an even worse disaster.

I reached Saint-Gervais and was reunited with my mother, who was overjoyed to see me. At eight o'clock that evening she called me to the kitchen.

'Come and listen to the BBC.'

'No thanks, Kiou, I'm off duty.'

I heard the wireless crackle, then, '*Ici Londres . . .*' Suddenly I gave a start. '*Message important pour Nestor: Jean très malade, ne retournez pas.*'

I was appalled. Five minutes later the message was repeated. I told my mother that I must get back to Corrèze immediately. She turned pale, but controlled herself with an effort.

'Look, I wanted to keep it a surprise, but your father told me he'd drop in tomorrow morning. Wait for him. He'll be a help. Besides, I don't see how you can leave tonight. There's no train.'

My father, who turned up the next day, was astonished to find me there. I told him I was catching the next train to Brive.

'I'll come with you,' he said promptly. 'It's always easier travelling as a twosome.'

We took the train to Fayet, changed at Lyons and headed for Brive. It was a very silent journey. I was shattered by the news, though I didn't know precisely what had happened. I only knew that I would have to make certain decisions in the next few hours – decisions that might affect not only the existence of the network but my personal freedom as well.

The train slowed, then pulled into the station at Quatre-Routes, the last stop before Brive. I gave a sudden start. My God, if I went on to Brive I was liable to be arrested on arrival. The station would be closely watched. Of course, the Verlhacs! Contact between networks was not recommended, but this was an emergency. It occurred to me that the message on the BBC might very well have come from George Hiller. I didn't know where George was, but I knew the Verlhacs by reputation. Jean Verlhac was the most loyal and devoted member of George's network.

'We're getting out,' I told my father quickly. He followed me out of the station. The Verlhacs were cheesemongers, and we found their house without difficulty. I rang the bell. The door was answered by a short woman with greying hair.

'Madame Verlhac?' I asked.

'Yes, monsieur. What can I do for you?'

'I'm Jacques, madame. I have to see George.'

Her suspicious gaze travelled from me to my father. At last she said, 'I don't understand. Who exactly is this George of yours?'

'Madame,' I said, 'I know I shouldn't have come here like this, but things are in a pretty bad way. I must see George.'

'Wait here,' she said. 'I don't know what you're talking about, but I'll call my husband.'

She shut the door and left us waiting there for a good five minutes. I heard voices inside the house, saw a curtain twitch. Then the door opened again and Jean Verlhac appeared. Having looked us up and down, he ushered us into the living room.

'I'm sorry,' he told me. 'Your friend must stay here. You, come with me.'

He showed me into his study. George was standing in front of the big fireplace, waiting for me. His expression was very grave.

'Your network has suffered a terrible setback. They've arrested Henri – also Delsanti, Bertheau, and Roland Malraux. Maurice Arnouilh had the same idea as you. He came straight to the Verlhacs, and Cyril Watney radioed a message to London. No doubt you heard it relayed by the BBC. Arnouilh went off, but he'll be back again in two days' time. What do you propose to do?'

'What do you think?' I replied. 'I'm going to rebuild the network, don't ask me how.'

'I didn't think you'd take it lying down,' George said, relaxing a little. 'London is very worried, though. To be quite frank, Buckmaster doesn't think you'll manage to evade the Boches for more than a day or two. They're watching Brive like hawks. They'd have nabbed you if you'd got out at the station. They've got a photo of you – a very poor likeness, fortunately, but they're beginning to plaster the walls of Corrèze with it. In short, the Gestapo are on the lookout for you everywhere. You know the form, don't you? The last message I had from London said I mustn't risk my own network, and I'd better steer clear of you.'

I not only knew the rules but thoroughly approved of them.

'You know I won't abandon you,' George went on, 'but we'll have to be ultra-careful. I'll inform London that we've retrieved you temporarily, and that you intend to pick up the pieces and carry on with Author's assignment. I'll also suggest that they communicate with you via Cyril – they call him Michel here. You can pass your messages through him if all goes well. Meantime, you'd better make yourself scarce, it's far too dangerous here. I'll give you a little money, too. Do you know where to go?'

1. Major Harry Peulevé, DSO, alias 'Jean' or 'Henri', head of the SOE's 'Author' network.

2. Captain Peter Lake, alias 'Jean-Pierre', arms instructor, and the author, 'Captain Jack'.

3. Major George Hiller, DSO, alias 'Maxime', head of the SOE's 'Footman' network.

4. Captain Ralph Beauclerk, alias 'Casimir', radio operator of the SOE's 'Nestor' network.

5. Colonel Robert Poirier, alias 'Robert', father of the author.

6. Captain Cyril Watney, radio operator and subsequently head of the 'Footman' network in succession to George Hiller, who was badly wounded.

7. 'Captain Jack' (*centre*) with Colonel Gaucher (*right*), alias 'Martial', departmental commander of the FFI.

'Don't worry,' I told him. 'I'll come back and find out what London says four days from now. If anything happens to me, the man outside will notify you.'

'Who is he?'

'My father, old boy.'

Peulevé's Peregrinations

Not far from the Lamories' house, where Henri and his team had just been arrested, stood a cottage occupied by a couple named Dufour. Dufour himself was a member of the Milice, and comings and goings at the Lamories' had caught his eye.

'If you ask me,' he told his wife, 'our neighbours are doing a bit of black-marketeering.'

More and more suspicious, he went to see Walter Schmald, who commanded the SD [Security Service] detachment at Brive and told him of his suspicions. The latter, notorious at Brive for his cruelty (he was executed after the war), was far more interested in capturing 'terrorists' than a few blackmarketeers.

A few days later, however, Schmald decided to pay the Lamories' house a visit, accompanied by four of his men. They drove there in two Citroën saloons, the first of which, with Schmald on board, pulled up almost in front of the house. The Germans piled out and made a dash for the front door, which proved to be unlocked. Hearing voices overhead, they raced upstairs. The rest was child's play – they arrested the room's four occupants in a matter of seconds – but Schmald was dumbfounded when he saw the transmitter. Instantly recognizing the exceptional nature of his haul, he could hardly conceal his glee, but he pulled himself together at once. He only had four men with him and the prisoners might well try to escape, so he proceeded with care. He herded them down the stairs with their hands up, opened the boot of one of the cars, and made Henri and Delsanti get inside. Bertheau was then installed in one car and Roland Malraux in the other. That done, Schmald ordered his convoy to head for Tulle. Doubtless he was feeling thoroughly pleased with himself.

* * *

After the war Henri Peulevé more than once told me how flabbergasted the Germans were to find themselves confronted by a group of *résistants*.

'You can just imagine,' he used to say. 'They'd have turned up in far greater numbers if they'd thought, even for one moment, that they were going to nab the members of a Resistance network.'

But Henri's principal emotion was fury at having been captured.

'You remember the routine,' he said. 'Every time we transmitted we used to post someone at the window to keep an eye on the neighbourhood. I myself had been standing at the window only a short time before. I don't know what happened. Four or five minutes' inattention? There were guns in that room – if we'd spotted them we'd have got the whole bunch. What a fiasco!'

Henri made himself ill, brooding about this tragedy, but there's no armour against fate. Disaster always strikes when one least expects it.

The Germans did not linger in Tulle for long. As soon as word of Schmald's precious haul reached them, the Gestapo at Limoges sent for his prisoners, so it was at the prison there that our friends spent their first night in captivity.

The next day, having undergone a relatively mild interrogation, they were transferred to Paris under close escort and separated. Henri Peulevé was taken to Fresnes Prison. I will not elaborate on the forms of torture to which he was subjected in Paris, especially at SD headquarters in the Avenue Foch, where he was half-drowned on several occasions. Despite these ordeals, Henri never disclosed any information of importance. The proof: no other member of the 'Author' network was arrested thereafter.

Though weakened physically, Henri preserved an iron determination and the hope that he would be able to escape. We did not remain idle at our end. I got in touch with some people who might possibly be able to help him escape from Fresnes. One day, while walking in the prison yard, Henri noticed that the door leading to the outer yard was unlocked. He pushed it open and tried to scale the second perimeter wall, hoping that freedom lay beyond it. He was clinging to the top of the wall when the Germans spotted him. A soldier opened fire, and Henri fell to the ground with a bullet in his leg. Without bothering to administer first aid, the Germans brutally hustled him back into his cell.

Henri's leg hurt badly. No one came to tend his wound, which was an ugly one, so the next day he decided to act. He took a small spoon and dug around. The pain redoubled in intensity, but after several attempts he managed to extract the bullet from his leg. Then he fainted.

Henri was limping when the Germans transferred him to the death camp at Buchenwald. He was not alone: more than thirty agents of the SOE and other special intelligence services were confined there too, including Yeo-Thomas, Maurice Southgate, George Wilkinson and Dubois Barrett.

Even in the camp they remained a close-knit group. On 6 September, 1944, fifteen of them were summoned to the commandant's office. They were never seen again. Three days later another sixteen received the same summons. They were never seen again either. The survivors resorted to a last, desperate expedient: two of them managed to contact Colonel Hans Ding-Schuler, the SS doctor in charge of medical experiments, and convinced him that, in order to save his own skin later on, he must save at least three of their number.

Schuler devised a plan. His service, which specialized in typhus problems, used to inoculate prisoners with the disease. His idea was to exchange the identities of three agents with those of three French inmates dying of typhus. The group chose Yeo-Thomas, Henri Peulevé, and Stéphane Hessel of the BCRA*, so Henri moved into the hut where Schuler conducted his 'experiments'. The Germans got wind of the affair and came looking for him. Meantime, one of the sick French prisoners died. Henri only just escaped execution by taking his place and assuming his identity. He became a Frenchman named Jean Chevalier.

The Germans took the dying man for Henri and registered his death in due course.

*Bureau Central de Renseignement et d'Action [Intelligence and Operations Branch], de Gaulle's counterpart of the SOE.

The real Jean Chevalier, who died so horribly in Buchenwald, was a young labourer who had refused to go and work in Germany with the STO, or compulsory labour service. His 'offence' being less grave than Henri's, he had been one of those prisoners who worked in gangs under guard outside camp.

Protected by their new identities, Henri and Yeo-Thomas were sent to work outside camp in one of these gangs. They both contrived to escape. Yeo-Thomas was recaptured first, but escaped again and managed to reach an American unit. Henri trudged through the countryside for hours until nightfall, when he sneaked into a nearby farmhouse. Taking a waistcoat and an old pair of civilian trousers from a cupboard, he stole out again without being spotted. He spent the night in some woods, where the distant sound of gunfire told him that Allied troops could not be very far away.

He awoke to find two SS men prodding his face with their submachine-guns.

'Who are you?' one of them demanded in a strong Belgian accent.

Henri didn't hesitate. 'I was working for the Germans. I'm trying to dodge the Americans. If they capture me they'll shoot me.'

'Don't worry,' the man told him, 'we're Belgian SS men. We're trying to get away too.'

Henri started chatting with his two new-found friends.

'You should get hold of some civilian clothes,' he told them. 'You'll find it easier to escape the Americans that way.'

'We've got some civvies in this bag,' replied one of the Belgians.

They put their guns on the ground, got out their civilian clothes, and started to pull off their uniform trousers. Henri snatched up the guns in a flash.

'I'm Major Henri Peulevé of the British Army,' he said coldly. 'You're my prisoners.'

I leave it to the reader to picture the look on the faces of the American soldiers who picked up an exhausted man – a walking skeleton barely able to stand – pushing two SS men ahead of him at gunpoint.

I regret my inability to give any details of how our other

comrades – Delsanti, Bertheau, and Roland Malraux – fared in the camps. Henri told me his own story a few weeks after surviving these tragic experiences. We were sitting in an unlit room in the south of France, having travelled through Dordogne and Corrèze, when he suddenly broke his silence and told me what I have recorded above – that and a great deal more besides.

We know that Delsanti and Roland Malraux were killed during the bombardment of Lübeck. This was a final outrage on the part of the Nazis, who put the most vulnerable prisoners – the survivors of the death camps – aboard some German ships in the harbour. Chained together, they were doomed to die in the cross-fire between Allied troops and the German defenders of the port.

Louis Bertheau met his death at Sandbostel, a camp near Bremen.

VI
THE 'NESTOR/DIGGER' NETWORK

I saw André Malraux again almost at once. He concealed the distress he felt at his brother's capture.

'I think we should meet often in the next few weeks,' he told me. 'I feel sure we can do some good work together.'

I agreed, but I also needed a little time if I was to try, as quickly as possible, to repair at least part of the edifice we had patiently constructed under Henri's leadership. Being actively sought by the Germans, I had to keep constantly on the move. And so, while resuming contact with the various maquis commanders, I made a point of never spending more than one night in the same place. I had joined forces again with Maurice Arnouilh, who accompanied me everywhere, and it was in his gas-fuelled car that we managed to pass so readily through incessant road-blocks and feel less prone to the disagreeable sensation that the net was closing around us. I was so wary that few people knew my whereabouts. Not even my father could always get in touch with me at this period. Proceeding with extreme care, I managed to resume contact with the Resistance and with Cyril Watney, whose radio remained my sole means of communication with London.

This way of life did not accord with the natural exuberance of our friend Maurice Arnouilh, whom we nicknamed 'le petit père génial' [the brilliant little fellow]. I realized that I would not be able to go on using his car indefinitely, and that I must find some other means of carrying out my work. The following incident became my pretext for severing contact with Maurice while remaining on the best of terms with him. Although he did not altogether understand my decision, it was dictated solely by considerations of security.

We set off for Martel, a place in Lot, where Maurice assured me that we could safely go to ground at a hotel owned by a friend of his. We got to the hotel, and my first impression, I must admit, was excellent. I retired to my room to have a bit of a rest and run over some air-drop particulars to be passed to Watney for transmission to London at the earliest opportunity. Maurice was waiting for me in the dimly-lit hotel restaurant when I came downstairs an hour later. He seemed at first to be on his own, but then I spotted a young man seated quietly at a nearby table. Not liking the look of him, I asked Maurice who he was.

'Just a nice young fellow who's trying to dodge his compulsory labour service. I've had a word with him – he's all right.'

I asked Maurice to follow me out into the hotel courtyard and impressed on him, for the umpteenth time, how careful we had to be.

'Just to make sure the youngster really *is* all right,' I said, 'I'm going to pay him a visit during the night. I'll get him to talk.'

Maurice was horrified. 'You can't do that,' he protested. 'What will my friend the *patron* think? We're quite safe here, believe me.'

'Very well,' I said. 'I won't go and hassle the youngster, but we'll leave at five tomorrow morning. Get the burner going in good time.'

We drove out of the hotel courtyard at five the next morning. Maurice took the road leading north to Corrèze, which was not far away.

I heard later that, just as we drove north, an armoured car accompanied by two Citroën saloons entered Martel from the south. One of the cars pulled up at the entrance to the village and the youngster from the hotel got in. He promptly led the SS men to the hotel and up to my room. Minangoix by name, he will reappear later on.

I was very preoccupied as we drove through Corrèze. I simply had to find some means of getting to Cyril Watney and passing him my list of air drops. All at once, as we rounded a bend, we were confronted by a German road-block. There was nothing to be done.

'*Raus, raus!*' the Germans yelled, and made us get out of the car with our hands up. We were dealing with ordinary

94

soldiers, I noticed, not SS men, and most of them had rather Asiatic features. (We found out later that they were Red Army men who had joined the Germans – Mongolians, I believe.) A sergeant examined our papers and seemed satisfied. I often changed names, and my documents came from a different source each time. On this occasion I was again travelling under the name of Jacques Perrier, timber merchant. My papers had been prepared by friends in the town hall at Périgueux, as I have already said, and looked thoroughly authentic.

Though seemingly satisfied, the sergeant decided to have some fun. He twice put us up against a wall and pretended to shoot us, but I managed to engage him in conversation.

'What are we supposed to have done?' I asked.

'Don't ask me. I'm waiting for my officer to come back. He's been gone an hour.'

'Why not let us sit in the car?'

'If you like,' he said with a smile. 'But it won't stop me shooting you if the officer gives the word.'

This was a vital move, because I had secreted the air drop papers under the carpet. We got back into Maurice's car with a soldier's rifle trained on us. I managed to retrieve the papers and slip them into my pocket. Then I hailed the sergeant.

'Mind if I stoke the burner?' I asked him. 'If you let us go the car won't move unless the gazogene is burning properly. If not, what's the difference?'

He shrugged. I got out and, with Maurice's assistance, lifted down the sack of charcoal we carried on the roof rack. We opened up the burner. While we were replenishing it, I extracted the papers from my pocket and added them to the fuel. I felt very proud of myself.

The officer returned. Having examined our papers, he found them so satisfactory that he actually removed his glove and shook hands with me.

'Continuez, messieurs,' he exclaimed. 'Weiterfahren!'

Maurice quickly resumed his place at the wheel and I jumped in beside him, but he was over-excited. He made a blunder while negotiating the road-block and landed us in the ditch. The Germans obligingly extricated us.

We continued on our way, thoroughly pleased with ourselves. A few kilometres further on I asked Maurice to pull up for a moment, wanting to see if anything remained of the papers in the burner. We opened it, only to discover that an updraft of some kind had deposited them, quite intact, on top of the charcoal!

Although I was very glad to have recovered them, I felt a retrospective pang of fear at the thought that the Germans might have asked us to open the door of the 'gazo'.

We should have been even more alarmed had we known that the Germans had gone to Martel to arrest us. Luckily for us, communications between Lot and Corrèze must have been poor that day.

This near-fatal incident convinced me of the need to split up for a while. I was sorry to leave Maurice, but the situation had become too tricky. Rather sadly, Maurice decided to join a group of friends in the neighbourhood of Ussel. As for me, I resolved to join Paul Lachaud at the Moulin du Cuzoul, his farmhouse near Daglan.

Maurice had been a wonderful companion. Brave and resourceful, he had probably saved my life by warning George Hiller of Henri's arrest, but I had no choice. It was essential that our network become operational again, and Maurice, for all his courage, was temporarily 'blown' and, thus, a threat to its security.

Before I went to see Lachaud, Maurice dropped me at Cyril Watney's command post so that I could pass him my messages for London concerning air drops. Then I made my own way to Poulou and Georgette. I stayed with them for several days, preparing for the drops that Watney had requested from London. I also wanted to find out how Raymond Maréchal was progressing with the organization of his small combat unit. Poulou sent word to him, and he came to Cuzoul at once. He enthusiastically explained his group's operational plans and mentioned someone called 'Soleil'.

'You must meet him,' he said, 'and his two sidekicks, Maurice and Michel.' He hesitated for a moment, then added, 'One can't fight a war with choirboys, you know. They're a bit wild, especially "Soleil", but you must meet them all the same.'

I did meet 'Soleil' soon afterwards. He was young – about my own age – but very high-spirited and endowed with a certain personal magnetism. I took to him.

Like everyone else, 'Soleil' was eager to get hold of some arms and mount spectacular operations as soon as possible. In the course of our conversation I told him that I was prepared to help provided I could rely on him to go into action promptly when the Allies gave the word. I added that I was fighting a war, and that any other matters – his organization and activities, for example – were of no concern to me as long as they did not endanger the Allies' plans. Finally, I confirmed that we would keep in touch through Raymond Maréchal.

I had every confidence in Maréchal. Although I felt faintly uneasy about 'Soleil', I considered that his group would prove very useful when augmented by Maréchal's men. I also formed a good impression of his two lieutenants, Maurice and Michel.

I left Cuzoul a few days later feeling satisfied with our organization, of which the Lachaud family would quickly become a staple and most effective part. I asked Poulou to take charge of the arrangements for our arms drops. Then I went to visit some maquis units in Corrèze, where I learned that Vincent Bonnetot had been reassigned by the FTP. I was disappointed at losing such a good friend and valuable associate.

Malraux, whom I saw again, informed me of his new contacts with the AS maquis of Dordogne and stressed how essential it was to speed up deliveries of arms by air. I told him that I had resumed regular contact with London, and that I was awaiting some more air drops.

I also went to the Verlhacs' for an important rendezvous with George Hiller, who gave me a warm welcome and produced a sheet of paper.

'Read this,' he said. 'It's from Buckmaster.'

The 'Author' network had been decapitated only two weeks before, but Buckmaster's message read as follows:

'Important message for Nestor *stop* You have just demonstrated your ability to carry on the work performed by Author *stop* As of now we appoint you head of a new network named Digger in direct succession to Author *stop* We will shortly be parachuting you an officer code-named Basil* as second-in-command and arms instructor and a radio operator code-named Casimir†

*Peter Lake, subsequently code-named 'Jean-Pierre'.
†Ralph Beauclerk.

97

stop Inform us soonest of your suggested landing site *stop* I send you my sincere congratulations *stop* You are promoted captain with effect from today.'

I was happy. It all showed that, thanks to my radio messages – and, no doubt, to a few kind words from Hiller, London realized that I had picked up the torch, and that the time had come to give me maximum support, both moral and material.

But in those days good news was invariably followed, almost at once, by disaster. Today was no exception. I was just drafting a message for London when Madame Verlhac burst into the room.

'There's a young woman asking for you,' she said breathlessly. 'Don't worry, I know her. It's Georgette Lachaud.'

I hurried out to see Georgette, who was pale and trembling. All she said was, 'The Germans caught Raymond. They shot him by the roadside.'

My friend Raymond Maréchal, one of the men who had risked death a hundred times in Malraux's squadron in Spain, had just met his death on a minor road not far from Domme, in Dordogne. He and his little group had run into a German ambush. Most of them were killed in the first flurry of shots, but Raymond was taken prisoner. The Germans forced him to put his hands on the glowing charcoal in his gazogene, then shot him. Thus died Raymond Maréchal the republican – 'a bit of an anarchist,' as André Malraux had called him.

Malraux was waiting for me at the Lachauds' in Cuzoul.

'We've taken another hard knock,' he said, 'but it's tragedies like these that will finally give birth to hope, because we're going to win through. With my connections I can help you a great deal. Not everyone agrees with me, but at least they'll listen to me. I am trusted by the members of the CNR⋆ in Paris. You, Jack, are in touch with London. You possess the requisite training for the fight that lies ahead and the facilities to arm those who wish to take part in it. I feel that an association between us could only be an asset to the Resistance. I suggest we go and spend a week in Paris. From your point of view it's essential. You're bound to be arrested if you remain here. For my part, I must clarify my position with the Resistance chiefs in Paris.'

⋆*Conseil National de la Résistance.*

I shared Malraux's wish for closer ties between us, because they could improve the co-ordination of the Resistance in our region and render it more effective. I made it clear, however, that I had no intention of renouncing my role as an expert adviser, and that I would never embroil myself in any problems directly relating to the command of the maquis.

I agreed to spend a few days in Paris. Malraux's suggestion apart, I thought I might be able to make an on-the-spot assessment of the chances of springing Henri from Fresnes Prison. I explained, however, that I could not make the trip right away because of the welcome news that I would very soon be getting a second-in-command and a radio operator of my own.

I also received a visit from 'Soleil', and, having no alternative, proposed that he replace Maréchal. He was already *de facto* in command of the group, because all Raymond's own recruits had died in the ambush. 'Soleil' did come up with one extremely useful suggestion: he offered to drive me to Siorac in Périgord.

'You'll meet Charles there. He's a highly resourceful type. You'll find him a great help. Besides, you'll be relatively safe at Siorac. They're all in the Resistance there.'

In consultation with Paul Lachaud, I arranged a landing site near Domme for Peter Lake and Ralph Beauclerk. We also took certain precautions relating to Cuzoul and the arms dump. I begged Paul and Georgette to be careful and not to sleep at the Moulin du Cuzoul, at least for the time being. Then I left for Siorac.

Charles the Bolshevik

Robert Brouillet, nicknamed Charles the Bolshevik, was a carpenter. Together with his wife Marguerite and his three children he inhabited part of a big house in the middle of Siorac known locally as 'the Château'. It was divided into two separate establishments: one housed Siorac's presbytery and its *curé*, the other Charles the Bolshevik and his family.

Whoever installed those champions of God and Marx under the same roof must have had a sense of humour – though in their case it was hard to know which of them was closer to the Almighty.

The Château de Siorac's vast and splendidly-proportioned hall functioned as a sitting-room, dining-room, and kitchen combined. It was, in fact, a communal living-room with benches flanking the big fireplace at the far end. In cold weather one could get warm by sitting inside the ingle-nook itself.

Charles, a man of about forty with work-worn features, was standing in the middle of the room when I entered. He made a grumpy, rather prickly impression, but this was belied by the look in his eyes, which radiated immense kindness. Paul Lachaud, who had accompanied me, introduced me as 'Jack l'Anglais' and started to say more, but our host cut him short and put out his hand.

'I'm Charles,' he said simply. He didn't invite me to sit down, just stared at me until I began to feel rather uncomfortable. His wife Marguerite, who was preparing some vegetables near the fire, glanced at me uneasily now and then. At last Charles broke the silence.

'I don't know you,' he said, still regarding me fixedly, 'but I'd better tell you, whether you like it or not, that I'm a Bolshevik and always will be.' He paused. 'Well, think you'll care to work with a Bolshevik?'

Looking at that decent, upright man, I realized why I was so immediately drawn to him. Smiling, I spoke for the first time since entering the room.

'Monsieur Charles,' I told him, 'I'm twenty-one and I'm fighting a war. Do you think I'd have had myself flown here from England if my sole concern were the deeply-held political beliefs of the people I've come to fight alongside? I'm a soldier. I don't care whether you're a Bolshevik or not. All I would ask you is this: Are we going to drive out the Boche together?'

Charles, clearly pleased with my reply, beamed. 'Sit here on my right,' he said. 'Marguerite, you can dish up the soup now.' And we sealed one of my life's most memorable friendships with generous platefuls of steaming *chabrol**.

Charles and Marguerite kept open house at the château. Any *résistant* who called there could count on getting a meal and a bed for the night, though how the admirable Marguerite managed

---

*It is an old custom in south-west France to add wine to the broth remaining at the bottom of a soup tureen and drink it straight from one's plate.

it was a mystery. The soul of integrity, Charles was not only discreet but absolutely disinterested.

Siorac was a little oasis of freedom. Its inhabitants, carefully supervised by Charles, who was no fool, had set up an efficient communications network. News of the approach of Germans, or even just of strangers, was promptly telephoned to the château by the local postmistress well before any such undesirables could get to Siorac itself.

Apart from conducting operations at Siorac, Charles demonstrated his resourcefulness in a multitude of ways – so many that I would be hard put to it to enumerate them all. You were looking for someone discreet and courageous to head a group? You needed a sound man with good local knowledge to help you select some landing sites? You wanted to locate some caches of arms or obtain accommodation for members of your network? There was only one answer to all such problems: Charles.

Such was the man who joined me just when I needed him most. His moral and logistical support was crucial to the success of our operations at this period.

Although he clung firmly to his political convictions, Charles was a pragmatist. One day I discovered that some of the arms we had asked him to hide for a while had been carefully deposited in the belfry of Siorac church.

'They're safe enough,' Charles told me with a wink. 'That God of yours is keeping an eye on them.'

He formed an ideal working relationship with Father Marchadoux, the *curé* of a neighbouring village, Sagelat, who was a former flyer and a genuine *résistant*, and the priest hid quantities of arms at his little church.

Charles's love of his neighbour was such that I have often thought the pact he formed was with Jesus Christ rather than Lenin.

In addition to helping me personally, he soon founded his own combat unit, the 'Castelréal' group, which we supplied with arms as a matter of course. Overtaxed by his manifold activities, he subsequently relinquished operational command of the group to Captain Leclerc, but he continued to be its inspiration and driving force.

Charles died in 1946. Paralysed and unable to speak, he was waiting for the end when his old friend Abbé Marchadoux, now *curé* of Siorac, came to see him. Suspecting that Marchadoux might still be secretly hoping to convert him. Charles managed, with a great effort, to shake his head. Very gently, he grasped the priest's hand by two fingers and raised them to his lips. Marchadoux understood the significance of the gesture. Producing a cigarette, he lit it and took a puff, then sealed their earthly friendship by putting it between Charles's lips.

My thoughts often turn to Siorac in Périgord. I have an abiding affection for the little town, but I shall never understand why its inhabitants have omitted to erect a monument or dedicate a street to a such a man.

The Coming of Casimir and Jean-Pierre

I remained at Siorac for several days. During that time I went to inspect the spot near Domme which Paul Lachaud had recommended as a landing site for 'Basil' and 'Casimir'. Though rather on the small side, it could be evacuated quite quickly once the air drop was over.

I entrusted Poulou with the arrangements and Charles the Bolshevik with overall charge of the 'reception committee'. The Germans were combing the district with increasing frequency, I emphasized, and speed would be essential when it came to hiding the two parachutists and retrieving the arms and money for which I was waiting so eagerly. I was particularly anxious to find some safe places for Casimir, my future radio operator, to transmit from. An operation like mine could succeed only if we maintained regular contact with London, and if messages in both directions could be transmitted without delay. The problem of communications was paramount, so our radio operator must be assured of maximum security. Knowing what had happened at Brive, I was determined that nothing of the kind should happen to my radio operator, even if I had to keep him a virtual prisoner and isolate him completely from the rest of the Resistance.

Malraux sent me a message asking to see me and inviting me over to his current abode near Castelnaud-Fayrac, so I paid him a visit. It was my first meeting with his companion, Josette Clotis. Malraux seemed perfectly content to lead a domesticated existence there, but I was impressed when he told me about his recent activities. He had managed to tour wide areas of Dordogne and establish contact with several maquis commanders, notably Bergeret, who was in charge of the south of the department. He stressed the urgent need for arms drops and the importance of our trip to Paris, being anxious to confer with some of the National Council's leading lights.

I returned to Siorac that evening to find Georgette Lachaud in tears. She told me that their farmhouse, the Moulin du Cuzoul, had been gutted.

Why? It seems likely that, after the skirmish in which Raymond Maréchal lost his life, the Germans had combed the environs of Daglan, Domme and Sarlat in search of other Resistance groups. What had inspired them to raid the farm? It was hard to tell. Incensed, perhaps, by the fact that Poulou and Georgette were not, luckily for them, on the premises, the Germans had set fire to their farm and then proceeded to amuse themselves by slaughtering their livestock. (They brutally decapitated all the ducks, hens and other poultry.) It was a severe blow, but the Lachauds were safe. What was more, they had removed our cache of arms a few days earlier.

At last we received a message over the BBC announcing the arrival of Casimir and Basil. It was set for the morrow, Easter Day, a good omen.

Charles and Poulou went on ahead to prepare the landing site. The moon was shining brightly by the time I joined them. It was a clear night – rather too clear for my liking. We heard the plane approach and saw it circle overhead. It was definitely far too visible for safety. I felt convinced that everyone in the district would spot it, the Germans included.

The plane lost height and circled the site in a wide arc. Poulou flashed the prearranged signal in Morse: A for Able. The crew couldn't fail to see it, the night was so clear. The plane flew right over our beacons, and we saw parachutes drifting down: a dozen-odd arms containers and two human figures. The men made an uneventful landing. I walked over to them.

I at once recognized Ralph Beauclerk, alias Casimir. We had met by chance while training – in fact we had even made a jump together at Ringway, the parachute training centre. A reserved, rather shy young man, he wore horn-rimmed glasses and looked more like an absent-minded professor than a secret agent. Just at present he was looking very nervous. Peter Lake, alias Basil, whose code-name was changed to 'Jean-Pierre' on arrival, was quite another type. A short man, he made a rather brusque impression and seemed to be a stickler for the rules. As soon as he landed he asked how long I thought it would take to evacuate the area and get them to a safe-house.

'The thing is,' he said, 'our instructions . . .'

'You mean instructions from London,' I cut in. 'Better forget them. Over here we make the best of what we've got, and what we've got is a clapped-out "gazo" van. It may or may not start on the button, I've no idea. Besides, I want to collect all those arms containers before they're filched by some of our well-meaning friends.'

Having got that off my chest I subsided, of course, and told my two new companions something of the conditions under which we operated. It wasn't always easy to apply the methods we'd learned in London.

'Take parachutes,' I said. 'You were taught to bury them, weren't you? Can you see them now? No, they've already vanished. They make splendid shirts for our maquisards.'

I have described this little episode without embellishment. In the event, Jean-Pierre became an outstanding second-in-command and a good friend – efficient, courageous, and full of humour. As for Casimir, who successfully established contact with London on arrival, he proved to be a radio operator of exceptional quality. The three of us made an excellent team – in fact we hit it off so well that André Malraux, who was sometimes tickled by our solidarity, christened us *'les farfelus'**, which to him was a compliment.

The 'gazo' did not start immediately, needless to say, and our two parachutists helped to push it like the rest. We went first to Charles's place, where Marguerite had prepared a little Périgord snack for the *'pauvres petits anglais'*.

Casimir took advantage of this brief respite to bring me up to date with developments in London and describe his departure. On arrival at Tempsford airfield, he and Peter Lake had been greeted by Vera Atkins and given a good meal. They were then conducted to a large room where all the

---

*Roughly, 'madcaps' or 'eccentrics'.

items and papers to be taken with them were carefully laid out on a table. They took off their uniforms and put on some civilian clothes ostensibly 'made in France'. After a final search, Casimir was handed the French money I so urgently needed and the secret codes for his transmitter. His account summoned up visions of my own 'infiltration' only months before, though it already seemed a lifetime ago: the flight, the threat of anti-aircraft fire, the long wait, the despatcher clipping our parachutes to the rail, the hole in the floor, the French countryside gliding past below us, the expectant thrill, the green light . . . It was all quite similar – except for one minor detail: they had been dropped in the right place!

I installed Casimir in an isolated country house belonging to a doctor from Luxembourg, and Poulou found another temporary abode for Jean-Pierre.

I informed the two newcomers that I would be away for several days and gave Casimir some messages for London, asking him to establish contact as soon as possible. I also instructed Jean-Pierre on his plan of action in the immediate future. That done, I rather reluctantly prepared to leave for Paris.

The trip struck me as important for several reasons. In the first place, as I have already said, it was not beyond the bounds of possibility that I would be able to do something for Henri and his comrades, who were still being held at Fresnes Prison. Secondly, I would have a chance to cement my relations with André Malraux and, with luck, make some valuable contacts in Paris. Last but not least, it could only be beneficial to my network and conducive to my personal safety if I made myself scarce for a while. On the other hand, the journey to Paris presented certain dangers in itself and I was uneasy at the prospect of abandoning my two Englishmen, if only for a few days. They were in good hands, however.

The Paris Trip

My plan was simple. I would first make for Limoges, where I possessed an excellent contact whose premises I had already used as a bolt-hole on more than one occasion. His story is worth telling.

On one of our trips together Maurice Arnouilh had mentioned Lucien Pons, a Limoges garage owner who had strayed into Pétain's *Légion* early in 1941, but had soon seen the error of his ways and was eager to help the Resistance. I badly needed a good hide-out in Limoges – and what could have been more ideal than the premises of one of Pétain's *Légionnaires*! – so I decided to go and see the man, who quickly convinced me of his honesty and sincerity. Pons was a First World War orphan, which may have accounted for his initial commitment to Pétain. He begged me to let him play an active part in the Resistance and was rather disappointed when I declined his offer. I asked him not to quit the *Légion*, but simply to put me up from time to time.

'Remain a good Pétainist,' I told him, 'and you'll be helping the Resistance.'

He finally agreed to let me have the run of a small but well-furnished apartment above his garage. Once in possession of the bunch of keys he gave me, I had acquired a wholly unsuspicious safe-house.

Lucien Pons was a great help to me at this period. Unfortunately for him, the Limoges FTP had no inkling of our relationship. Under the impression that he was a collaborator, they bombed and badly damaged his garage when Limoges was liberated. I came to his rescue and enlightened the FTP authorities on his services to the Resistance.

I duly arranged to join Malraux on board the Paris train at Limoges. He suggested taking a girl with us, namely Flora, who was one of our liaison officers and acted as a courier between us.

'She'll be a great help,' Malraux told me. 'You can play at being a young married couple in the train – much better for you than travelling alone. Her papers are impeccable and she's pretty, so you shouldn't have any trouble with the police or the Germans. When we get to Paris she'll catch a train to the Dordogne and inform Lachaud that the journey went all right.'

My father, 'Commandant Robert', visited Siorac just before I left. He'd had a few problems, but he told me that he would be free to join my group in two weeks' time. Meanwhile, he was going to Paris to look up some contacts who might prove useful to Henri, though he wasn't too optimistic. After that he had to go to Rennes for a couple of days. I explained that I was also going to Paris, and we arranged to meet at the Rond-Point, the Champs-Élysées roundabout, at noon the following Wednesday.

I left for Limoges. All went well until I ran into a serious check-point at the platform exit. The station was swarming with Germans and French militiamen.

'Papers,' said a German.

I produced my identity card. He examined it, handed it back, and waved me through. The militiaman beside him was staring at me oddly. I walked calmly on, bag in hand, but my heart was thumping: the militiaman was following me. I felt an overwhelming urge to run, but I suppressed it. The concourse was crowded. Abruptly, I turned off right and hid behind a column. The militiaman walked straight on. I waited awhile, then emerged without seeing him. Pons's garage was near the station. Having made a long detour for safety's sake, I went into a café and telephoned him.

'No problem,' he said. 'I'll meet you outside the garage.'

I spent a pleasant evening in the apartment above the garage, where Pons joined me with the makings of an excellent meal. Before leaving he offered to escort me to the station next morning.

'Your train leaves at eight,' he said. 'I'll pick you up and drive you to the station at the last minute. Don't worry, I can come and go freely there. We'll have no trouble getting through, not with my papers. You won't have to hang around the station before you leave.'

The next morning he picked me up at the garage and drove me to the station with only minutes to spare – in fact I was afraid of missing my train. Pons, brandishing a tricolour identity card, greeted a couple of militiamen in passing and saw me into a carriage just before the train pulled out. A man at the far end of the same carriage was trying to attract my attention. It was Malraux, sneezing, eyes running. He looked nervous.

'What happened?' he whispered.

'Nothing,' I replied, laughing. 'I'm here, aren't I?'

'I think it would be wiser not to travel together. We'll sit in different compartments, but we can always have an occasional chat in the corridor.'

I was about to enter a compartment when he shook his head.

'Not that one,' he told me with a smile, indicating the compartment next door. 'Go and sit with Flora.'

Once inside, I found myself alone with a very pretty girl. Flora had made herself look particularly stunning for the occasion. I sat down beside her, prepared to play the role of her husband with a will, but our liaison officer was not only a sensible girl: she was engaged into the bargain!

Flora married her fiancé, a fellow *résistant* named Lescot, just before the Liberation. Tragically enough, the brave young couple were killed in a car crash while on honeymoon.

After half an hour Malraux got bored and joined us.

'You know,' he said, peering this way and that, 'this war is going to be won by America alone, not only by force of arms but on the cultural plane as well, and very decisively. America was powerful already, and the war will multiply her power by ten. It was the Napoleonic epic that paved the way for British supremacy, don't forget. It's the same thing all over again. The Nazis are going to hasten America's rise in the world. You know the old joke?' he said, looking at Flora. 'Surely you do. Hitler is defeated and surrenders to Roosevelt, Churchill and Stalin, who discover, on reflection, that they owe him their increased power. At that moment Hitler tears off his moustache, comes to attention, and introduces himself: "Colonel Lawrence!"'

Malraux sighed. 'Ah, Lawrence . . .' he said, and promptly proceeded to dissect *Seven Pillars of Wisdom*. It was Malraux at his best – an enthralling exposition of a book that had affected me deeply – and I listened with close attention. Suddenly he broke off.

'By the way,' he said, 'do you also propose to play Lawrence and impose Britain's views on our *résistants* once the Boches have been sent packing?'

I laughed. 'Be serious, André, I've no intention of playing Lawrence. I came to fight a war and help the French to liberate themselves. I shall leave as soon as it's all over, and that's what my bosses think too. My job is quite straightforward: I'm here to help the Resistance as much as possible, mainly by organizing air drops of arms and equipment, and to assist in the recruitment of partisans to carry out guerrilla operations before and after the Allied landing. In return, I have to be satisfied that systematic acts of sabotage and attacks on enemy lines of communication will be launched on D-Day, either by the maquis or by small teams of specialists. Anything else, like political interference, is taboo. I couldn't care less about French politics. You have to be Gallic to believe that.'

I must have sounded most convincing, because Malraux shot me one of his characteristic friendly glances. Was he thinking that, for an Englishman, I cherished a peculiarly soft spot for France? Quite possibly.

There was a brief silence. Then he was off again. 'The communists are like the *curés*,' he said, drawing an imaginary square in the air. (In his mind's eye this square must have signified a narrow-minded prisoner of principle.) He broke off. The train was slowing.

'It's Vierzon, the demarcation line,' he said. 'I'm going back to my compartment.'

Flora, dutifully resuming work, came and sat close beside me. Two Germans and a ticket inspector entered the compartment. Flora nestled still closer with my hand lovingly clasped in hers. The inspector checked our tickets. One of the Germans scrutinized my interzonal travel permit and other documents. Then, with a faintly sarcastic '*Bon voyage*', the three of them left the compartment.

I waited a few minutes before joining Malraux in the corridor. He pointed out that quite a few people had got on at Vierzon.

'The next stop is Aubrais-Orléans. A lot more passengers will join the train there, take it from me, so you'd better stay in your compartment. When we get to Paris, follow me at a safe distance. Make your exit with Flora, then leave her and continue to follow me. I shall take the Métro to Gallimard. Wait outside for me. I won't be long, but I'll have fixed you up with somewhere to stay by the time I reappear.'

We were approaching Aubrais, so I left him and went back to Flora. It was high time, because the train soon came to a stop and a lot of passengers got in. Our compartment quickly filled up. There were plenty of Germans as well as civilians, but none of them gave me a second glance.

I arrived in Paris with very mixed feelings. I was going to see the French capital again for the first time since 1939, but the prospect of seeing it under German occupation troubled me greatly. Flora gave me an odd look, and I controlled my emotions with an effort. We emerged from the station arm in arm. A few steps further on I said, 'Tell Jean-Pierre that everything's all right. Have a safe trip back, and see you soon.'

I left her rather abruptly, anxious not to lose sight of Malraux, who was bustling along ahead of us. He descended the Métro steps. I was about to follow suit when I saw him hurry up them again. I turned on my heel in the crowd. He caught me up.

'There's a spot-check in progress down there,' he whispered.

He seemed to know the district well, because a few minutes later we came to another Métro station. I had difficulty in keeping up, lost sight of him, and panicked, having forgotten to ask him where to get out for Gallimard. I had to find him again. Just as I got into the train I caught sight of him in the next carriage. It really felt as if I were back in England, learning how to tail someone – or rather, learning how to give a tail the slip. Malraux signalled that he would be getting off at the next stop. I got the impression that he was sick of all these precautions, and I was right. No sooner had I set foot on the platform than he breezed straight up to me.

'That's it,' he said. 'I've had enough of these crazy gymnastics.' And he went on to talk about an exhibition of paintings he simply had to see.

'I'll be careful, but I've absolutely got to see it.'

We walked to Gallimard's office building.

'Go for a stroll, Jacques. I'll meet you here in twenty minutes.'

Outside the door he paused to shake hands warmly with a man who was just emerging, then walked off with him. He didn't go into the publisher's offices at all. I was rather uneasy, wondering what he could be up to, but decided to go for a stroll all the same. Suddenly I passed the man Malraux had just greeted, turned round, and saw that he was merely returning to the offices from which he had emerged five minutes earlier. As for Malraux, he had disappeared.

I continued my stroll and returned to the intersection of rue de l'Université and rue de Beaune. Malraux was there. We didn't linger long. Two men a little older than I but younger than Malraux were crossing the street. Malraux indicated the one on the left.

'Camus,' he said.

He didn't introduce the other man, whom he seemed not to know. Camus gave his companion a look of inquiry. 'Is it all right?'

The man nodded, then turned to me and said, 'Ten tonight, on the platform of the Sablons Métro station at Neuilly.' He added, 'You know Neuilly?'

I could hardly tell him that I had been born and raised there. I nodded, and we parted company. Malraux went off with Camus.

The weather was glorious, not cold at all. I had grown tired of chasing after someone else. Now I was my own master, alone at last with no one to follow.

At ten that night I got out at Sablons station. The man I had met was sitting on a bench on the platform. He got up, walked past me and out into the avenue. I followed him through the neighbourhood I knew so well from my childhood. He turned right down a side street. There was no one tailing us. He turned left and left again. Still no one. He paused outside a house, checked to see that I was following, and went in. The door was open when I reached it, but the interior was in darkness. A hand drew me inside and propelled me along a passage.

'Fifth floor,' said the man. He sounded rather edgy. Before we started up the stairs he told me, 'If we bump into anyone, you're a cousin of mine from the provinces. We met by chance. The hotels were full and you didn't know where else to go. It's very cramped, I warn you, especially as my wife has just had a baby. That takes up some room.' He added, 'Don't worry, it'll be all right.'

We reached the apartment at last. A passage, a kitchen on the right, some doors. There were people behind them, no doubt, but they didn't show their faces. Finally, a door on the left. We went in. It was cramped right enough. There was a young woman, a cradle (we whispered so as not to wake the baby), and one solitary bed.

My host turned to his wife. 'This is . . .' He looked at me inquiringly.

'Jack,' I said.

'Jack,' he repeated. His wife apologized for the lack of room. I wondered how we were going to manage. In the end we put the mattress on the floor for her while I and her husband shared the bedsprings.

We spoke very little. I felt worried at having descended on this nice young couple out of the blue. They seemed quite unaware that they were risking their lives for a total stranger. If I were captured on the premises, they would undoubtedly be shot. It was insane.

The baby, a little girl, woke up for her bottle. She caught sight of me and stared wide-eyed, the way babies do. Then she smiled at me.

'Her first smile!' the mother exclaimed. 'She's only two weeks old. She's never smiled before. What a good omen!'

I almost got up and left – the thought that this baby might suffer on my account was hard to endure – but I ended by falling asleep.

I was the last to wake, doubtless roused by the aroma of coffee. My hosts marvelled at me.

'You're an incredibly sound sleeper,' I was told. 'We spent all night at the window – a regular firework display. It simply didn't stop. News travels fast. This morning we heard they clobbered the marshalling yard at Villeneuve-Saint-Georges. Not much left of it, apparently. No station, no trains running.'

The thought of being stuck in Paris irritated me, but the husband broke in on my thoughts. 'We'll expect you around the same time tonight,' he said. I smiled at him. Small though the room was, I felt at home there, perhaps because it was so long since I had experienced a family atmosphere.

'If I'm going to have to impose on you again I'll let you know this afternoon,' I said, and took my leave. I had arranged to meet Malraux in the Champs-Élysées at eleven and my father at the Rond-Point at noon.

Having plenty of time in hand, I strolled up the Champs-Élysées. Although I bristled every time a German military vehicle drove past, I remained calm. The night's sleep had done me good and I felt invigorated as I walked up the broad, sunlit avenue. At the mouth of rue Pierre-Charron, or so I seem to recall, stood a pet shop with a window full of dogs and puppies in cages. To kill time I went in and looked at the animals. All at once, from the back of the shop, came a succession of furious barks. I went to investigate and saw a magnificent Alsatian hurling itself at the door of its cage. Men who have been living under intense pressure for months are prone to sudden impulses, and I was no exception. Strange as it may seem, I felt that I had just met a kindred spirit. I called an assistant and asked him to open the cage.

'Out of the question, monsieur, it's a ferocious animal – wants to bite everyone. We don't know what to do with it.'

'Just open the door a little,' I said, politely but firmly. With great reluctance, the man opened the door a few inches. I don't know what possessed me, but I put my hand through the gap. The dog stopped barking at once and licked it.

'It's fate,' I said.

The shop assistant stared at me. 'What did you say, monsieur?'

'Nothing, nothing,' I said, 'but if you've got a good, strong lead I'll take him off your hands.'

And that was how Dick entered my life and joined the Resistance.

I was hardly out of the shop before I realized what a monumental blunder I'd made. I was a wanted man. I had to avoid drawing attention to myself, and here I was, scheduled to meet Malraux in a few minutes' time and leading a huge Alsatian down the Champs-Élysées at ten-thirty in the morning.

Malraux duly turned up. I had never seen him like that before. Wide-eyed and open-mouthed, he stared first at me, then at Dick. He was absolutely thunderstruck.

'What,' he said at last, 'is *that*?'

'A dog, André.'

He relapsed into silence for a moment. Finally he said, in his harsh voice, 'You really are a *farfelu*.' Promptly forgetting all about Dick, he went on to tell me about the contacts he had made. 'I'm seeing some National Council members tonight. It's important. I suggest we fix another rendezvous for tomorrow. Let's meet on the *quai* opposite Notre-Dame. We'll go and have some lunch together.' He glanced at Dick and opened his mouth to say something, but I cut him short.

'Don't worry, André. Tomorrow I'll come on my own.'

'Fine. How's it going with Lescure?'

Camus had filled him in about the couple who were putting me up. He disclosed that the husband's name was Jean Lescure, and that he was one of the *résistants* in charge of clandestine printing and publishing. I told Malraux that my hosts were remarkable people, but that I had no wish to abuse their hospitality or endanger a family with a baby a few weeks old. Besides, I said, their place was too small.

Malraux concurred. 'Bring your bag tomorrow, I'll have found you somewhere else by then,' he told me. 'It's too late to do anything about tonight.' He confirmed his intention of paying a call on my hosts that afternoon, so we arranged to meet again at three and go out to Neuilly together.

I left Malraux and went to keep the appointment with my father, whom I shall henceforth call Commandant Robert. I found him calmly waiting for me at the Rond-Point, but he was quite as taken aback as Malraux had been to see my four-legged friend. Dick had already grown admirably accustomed to his new life and was in fine fettle. The only problem was that he seemed to have an aversion to German uniforms, and there were plenty of those on the Champs-Élysées in spring, 1944!

I had left it to Robert to get in touch with some people who might be able to help us to spring Henri from Fresnes. He gave me an account of his meetings with those rather shady individuals.

'The news isn't good,' he told me. 'For one thing, I don't trust them. For another, I haven't even managed to discover if Henri is still at Fresnes. I wouldn't bank on it, but they've promised to embody some more information in a semi-coded letter and mail it to an address I maintain outside your network.'

It was all very disheartening. Anxious though I was to get Henri out of prison, we had to be exceedingly careful. The people in question were a bunch who had dealings with the Germans, and they could well have betrayed us for the sake of some favours from the Gestapo.

Robert gave me news of Kiou and my brother, then turned his attention to Dick.

'You really can't go on traipsing around Paris with that animal of yours,' he said uneasily. 'Why not let me have him for the time being? An older man walking a dog isn't half as conspicuous. I've got to go to Brittany, true, but I'll take him with me and deliver him to you at Siorac ten days from now.'

'Just what I hoped you'd say,' I said, and prepared to take my leave.

I had reckoned without Dick, who had no wish to be parted from me, his new-found friend. Much to the amusement of a large crowd of bystanders, he kicked up an incredible fuss in the middle of the Champs-Élysées before reluctantly allowing himself to be led off.

I spent a second night with the Lescures. The next morning, after bidding farewell to Madame Lescure and the baby, I accompanied Jean into town. I left him near the Opéra, but not before thanking him warmly for his hospitality.

'See you again soon, I hope,' he said.

'That's a promise,' I told him. 'When Paris is liberated, I'll come and give your baby a kiss.'

As the reader already knows, and as I am ashamed to admit, I did not see Jean Lescure again for another thirty-five years, and even then the circumstances of our reunion were almost as fortuitous as those that led to our first meeting.

I killed time while waiting for my second rendezvous with Malraux by strolling along the boulevards. Outside the Madeleine I had an unexpected encounter. During my time in London I had met a charming young woman who belonged to the same service. In fact I had taken her out a couple of times and found her a delightful companion. We were both preparing for our respective missions, however, so I did not see her immediately prior to my departure. And now, here she was outside the Madeleine, evidently waiting for someone. Instructions from London were that agents belonging to different networks should show no sign of recognition while in France. Remembering this just in time, I regretfully passed her by. She recognized me at once and gave a covert smile.

'God bless you, Violette,' I said quietly, and went on my way.

Violette Szabo, the young widow of a French officer and a member of the SOE, was parachuted into France. Captured and tortured by the Germans, she was consigned to a concentration camp and died there. Her tragic story is told in the film *Carve Her Name with Pride* (1958).

Malraux beamed when he saw me, though I suspect that Dick's absence had something to do with the warmth of his welcome.

'The National Council is thinking of appointing me to co-ordinate the Resistance movements in Lot, Corrèze and Dordogne,' he announced. 'They're meeting tomorrow to decide. I'll have plenty on my plate, but it can only benefit our own work together. Now let's go and eat. We'll have to be careful, though, I can't afford to be recognized.' He mopped his eyes and sniffed. 'You really put the wind up me with that dog of yours, you *farfelu* . . . All right, let's take the Métro.'

I accompanied him down the steps. He was in great form, talking volubly and waving his arms about as if quite unconscious of the risk we were running. He was André Malraux, the literary lion, once more. We boarded a train and stationed ourselves near the door. Malraux was untroubled by the proximity of two German naval officers at my elbow. He proceeded to give me his views on the military situation.

'The Germans are finished. They lost the war at Stalingrad. The Russian advance is going like—'

'André,' I hissed, 'they'll hear you!'

He frowned at me. 'They obviously didn't teach you anything about acoustics at school.' I stared at him open-mouthed, but he went on, 'Given our present location, the only place we can be heard from is those two seats at the far end on the right, and they, as you can see, are currently unoccupied. There's absolutely no danger of being overheard.' He broke off suddenly. 'Ah, this is where we get out.'

I couldn't have been more delighted to get out. We were near the Place de la Concorde. All at once, Malraux seemed to change his mind.

'Come on, let's do ourselves proud. We'll go to Prunier's.'

'Surely they know you there?' I protested.

'Not as well as all that,' he said airily.

He led the way into Prunier's. The maître d'hôtel came bustling up with a broad smile.

'*Bonjour*, Monsieur Malraux.'

8. Madeleine Bleygeat, courier of the 'Nestor'/'Digger' network.

9. Air drop in south-west France.

10. *Left to right*: Lieutenant Christian Placais; André Malraux, alias Colonel Berger *(back to camera)*; ?; Captain Paul Lachaud, alias 'Poulou'. Inter-Allied Headquarters, Lot, Corrèze, Dordogne.

11. On the steps of the Palais de Justice, Périgueux, during the official visit of Colonel Maurice Buckmaster in 1947; (*left to right*) Lieutenant Colonel Boilet ('Gisèle'); Colonel Buckmaster (head of SOE's French section); Préfet Maxime Roux; Major Bourne Patterson; Colonel RE Poirier ('Commander Robert'); Major Jacques Poirier ('Martial'). (*Placais collection*).

12. The author receives his diploma of honorary citizenship from Jean Charbonnel, the Mayor of Brive-en-Gaillarde. On the same occasion, he presented the town with documents embodying the surrender terms under which Brive was liberated from the Germans on 15 August, 1944.

13. Her Majesty the Queen Mother receives M. and Mme Jacques Poirier in March, 1984. (*Imperial War Museum*).

The restaurant was full of Germans and their French confederates. I found it hard to swallow the first few mouthfuls of my excellent lunch, but Malraux was in a sunny mood.

'I have a date with someone on the *quais* near here,' he told me when lunch was over. 'I'll be gone a good hour. After that I'll take you to your new quarters.' Then he had a better idea. 'On second thoughts, come with me. You'll be interested.'

I had some time to spare, so I went with him. The *quais* were almost deserted. We walked beside the Seine for a few minutes. Then Malraux's 'date' turned up. It was Camus. He greeted me warmly and asked if all had gone well at the Lescures'. He had found me an ideal hideout, he said, but I couldn't move in there until tomorrow.

'Tonight you can sleep at Jean Paulhan's.'

I became aware that my lodgings were ultimately Camus's concern. He then launched into a long conversation with Malraux. Although I assumed a highly attentive and knowledgeable air, I'm bound to admit that, being very young and having little experience of their intellectual circle, I was defeated by much of what passed between Malraux and Camus that afternoon beside the Seine. Our toings and froings must have covered a good five kilometres. Sometimes I walked between them, sometimes on Camus's right, sometimes on Malraux's left, and all the while the words flowed back and forth.

Malraux: 'Man amounts to nothing in the face of death.'

Camus: 'All true writers know the value of human life.'

I felt as if I were listening to a BBC broadcast being jammed by the Germans. Snatches of conversation came to my ears: 'The war . . .' – jamming – 'Lenin held that joint action is always permissible, but you must never get your flags or words of command muddled . . .' – more jamming – 'China . . . Algeria . . . Stalingrad . . .' It was magnificent in its way, but! Not only did the two men appear to understand each other perfectly, but, like true gentlemen, they seemed to grant each other an equal share of the time available for speech.

They had been scintillating for a good two hours when Camus broke off in mid-sentence and turned to me.

'Time to go,' he said. 'We must take you over to Paulhan's.'

'Paulhan,' Malraux explained, 'is the literary director at Gallimard. He has to tread carefully, but he's a true *résistant*. Tomorrow I'll come and take you to your new quarters.'

Camus and Malraux accompanied me to rue des Arénes, where Paulhan himself answered the door. He briefly greeted my two companions but did not invite them in. I found myself alone with him.

Paulhan led the way upstairs. A man of medium height, he had a rather squeaky voice and seemed thoroughly ill at ease.

'This is a very risky business,' he said. 'The Germans are watching me. I could get myself arrested, but still . . .'

On the third floor he ushered me up yet another flight of stairs and into a kind of attic. There was a bed in one corner and an incredible number of canvases propped against the walls. Paulhan indicated them with a sigh.

'Braques and Fautriers,' he said. 'I keep them hidden away because of the Germans. If they show up you can always sneak off across the roofs, and good luck to you, but my poor pictures . . .'

It was clear that Paulhan, the *éminence grise* of clandestine literature, valued his pictures a great deal more highly than my humble person, but I took to him in spite of his strangely apprehensive and unwelcoming manner. He lingered in the attic for some time, showing me his favourite canvases. At last he came out with it.

'You may think me unduly cautious, but I was arrested back in 1941. I belonged to a network. They released me, but it was no joke. I'll leave you now, but I'll bring you a snack in an hour or two. Have a good night's sleep. Your friends will collect you tomorrow. You'll be all right. You're going to Gide's.'

Neither Malraux nor Camus had mentioned that my next port of call would be André Gide's Paris apartment. I knew that Gide was in North Africa, so I wondered aloud who my host would be. 'You'll find out in due course,' was all Paulhan could tell me.

When Malraux came to collect me he said that things were going well, but that he would be out of touch for the next two days.

'I suggest we rendezvous in the Limoges train on Monday. By the way, I bumped into a friend of mine from Corrèze. It seems your trip to Paris has done the trick. There's a rumour that you've left the district and gone to England or Spain. I'm pretty sure the Germans will have got wind of it – an excellent thing from your point of view. It shows how right I was to insist on your coming here. Now I'll take you to Gide's, or rather, introduce you to someone who'll take you there.'

Paulhan was out, so I had no chance to thank him for his hospitality. We met up with the person who was to take me to Gide's apartment. Malraux briefly introduced me, then left us. My guide didn't tell me his name.

'We're going to rue Vaneau. You'll be fine there. The only snag is, you mustn't open the shutters. The apartment is supposed to be unoccupied. A woman will bring you your meals, and I must ask you not to leave the building. We don't want the concierge to spot you.'

'You mean I'm a prisoner?' I asked with a smile.

He laughed. 'In a manner of speaking, but it's a very nice prison.'

We entered the building as unobtrusively as possible and made our way up to Gide's apartment. My guide produced a key and let us in. I couldn't see a thing.

'Wait,' he said, 'I'll switch on some lights. Keep them to a minimum at night, though.'

I found myself in a room remarkable for its appearance as well as its vast size. The apartment was a kind of duplex, the walls upstairs being lined from floor to ceiling with bookshelves. I'd never seen so many books.

'You won't be short of reading matter,' my guide said rather derisively.

'Couldn't be better,' I told him. 'I haven't done much reading lately.'

The man wished me a pleasant stay and left. I climbed the little spiral staircase to the library and surveyed the shelves, feeling quite overwhelmed.

'Here I am in the library of one of France's greatest living writers,' I told myself. 'I'm actually staying at his apartment. Life is fascinating, no doubt about it.'

My contemplation of all those wonderful books was interrupted by the appearance of an old woman carrying a tray.

'Your lunch,' she said, depositing the tray on a small table, and promptly disappeared.

I must have devoted at least twenty-four of the forty-eight hours I spent in Gide's apartment to reading and browsing through his books. I also slept a little and on one occasion, although curiosity is a reprehensible failing, opened the shutters a couple of inches. I was staggered by the sight that met my eyes. The window overlooked a large courtyard guarded by uniformed sentries, and in the middle of the courtyard I caught sight of Pierre Laval, administrative head of the Vichy government and second in line to Marshal Pétain. Half regretting that I didn't have a rifle with me, I carefully closed the shutters again. I learned later that Gide's apartment adjoined the Hôtel Matignon, which at that time was Laval's residence when he visited Paris.

Cultural adventures apart, I was growing very bored in Paris and felt that I ought to return to the south-west as soon as possible. My brief vacation had doubtless done me good and thrown the Germans off the scent. That said, I had to get back to my team, so I decided to catch the first available train the next day, with or without Malraux.

That afternoon the guide paid me a visit. I took advantage of his presence to ask him to inform Malraux of my forthcoming departure. He told me he would do his best, though he wasn't sure if he could get in touch with him at such short notice. So saying, he made an unobtrusive exit.

I got to the Gare d'Austerlitz and was about to board my train when I caught sight of Malraux on the platform. He made a beeline for me.

'I quite understand,' he said. 'They let me know. I'm coming too. I've got a lot to tell you.'

We installed ourselves in a deserted compartment. Malraux coughed, blew his nose, wiped his eyes, gave a resounding sniff, and finally, after treating me to a long, portentous look, made the following announcement: 'From now on, my dear Jack, I'm Colonel Berger.'

'Fine,' I said inanely, finding it hard to keep a straight face.

'I've seen all the members of the National Council and they've formally confirmed my appointment. I'm to co-ordinate Resistance operations in Lot, Corrèze, and Dordogne. In practical terms,' he added, 'my job is to coordinate relations between the various groups and weld them into a unified command. You can help me in several ways: first, by informing us of the Allies' main objectives and thereby rendering the maquis more effective; secondly, by setting up a kind of military training school with your lieutenants; and thirdly, of course, by arranging air drops. The other systems just aren't working. You're the only one with the facilities to organize them properly.'

I had listened with interest to this exposé from the newly-fledged Colonel Berger.

'André,' I said, 'what are you going to do about General de Gaulle's representatives – the DMRs* and so on?'

'Do you see much of them?' he asked quickly.

I was forced to admit that I'd never yet met any DMRs and had no idea if the maquis kept in regular touch with them.

Malraux's projected attempt to co-ordinate operations struck me as an admirable idea, and it did not seem absurd that he should have been assigned such a task by the people he had just conferred with. The unification of the various Resistance movements was a strategy in line with the one Jean Moulin had essayed at national level.

I thought it an excellent thing that people like Malraux had decided to play a leading role. His charismatic personality, enthusiasm and contempt for danger would be of great assistance to us, now that the time was approaching when we would have a major part to play in the liberation of France. I didn't question the validity of his mandate. We were living in very exceptional times, and I had seen many a courageous, dynamic man proclaim himself leader of this group or that. Well, why not, provided he was capable of sustaining his self-imposed burden of responsibility? We were at war, and war precluded the hierarchical considerations of seniority and promotion so dear to our civil servants.

'Colonel Berger' would not have much authority to begin with, but General de Gaulle had even less when he penned the following words in June, 1940:

'As for me, with a hill like that to climb, I was starting from scratch. I possessed nothing whatever in the way of an armed

*Délégués Militaires Régionaux [Regional Military Delegates]

force or organization. In France, no backing and no reputation. Abroad, neither credit nor standing. But this very deficiency outlined my course of action. It was by unstinted devotion to the cause of national salvation that I would manage to acquire authority.'

Great men must sometimes give destiny a nudge. Although Malraux's personal commitment was not, of course, on a par with de Gaulle's, both men were leaders and made no bones about the fact. If Malraux/Berger gave destiny a little nudge in April, 1944, he did so for the good of the Resistance.

It seemed to me that Malraux's suggested alliance could prove of benefit to all concerned. My own contributions to our 'marriage' might be greater − contacts with London, a close-knit organization and arms drops were tangible assets − but Malraux was contributing Colonel Berger, or, rather, Colonel Berger was lending us Malraux.

That was how, in the train that was taking us to the south-west, we formed the association that someone would later christen 'Inter-Allied Headquarters'.

I had several reasons for satisfaction when I got back to Siorac. Charles and 'Poulou' Lachaud had done a great job reconnoitring landing sites, Casimir was successfully maintaining regular contact with London by radio, and Jean-Pierre had been instructing maquis units in the use of air-dropped arms and explosives.

My little team was already operational. Jean-Pierre had been sent to me as an arms instructor, but his sang-froid and sense of humour were such that, as the scope of our operations increased, I soon considered appointing him my deputy. Though somewhat inflexible, he was amply endowed with common sense, and I realized, when he told me how he had fared with the maquis unit commanded by 'Soleil' at Villefranche in Périgord, that he was rather clumsily expressing what I had felt for some weeks. The agreement I had reached with 'Soleil' after Maréchal's death could not survive for much longer, that much was certain. He was too unreliable, too fiercely independent, and the image he projected alarmed me at times. I hesitated for all that, because I was fond of the fellow in spite of the reproaches I could have levelled at him. He was about my own age, and we should have been able to hit it off. Extremely courageous, he was persuasive and likeable into the bargain.

He also had two lieutenants with whom I had got on well. One of them was Maurice Nusenbaum, a coldly efficient operator. The other, Lucien Gambelon, was a brave and indomitable *résistant* who decided to join me when my relations with 'Soleil' became strained.

'Soleil' did render me one last service: he introduced me to Fernande Vidalie de Castelnaud-Fayrac, nicknamed Nandoue. A schoolteacher whose husband was a prisoner in Germany, she had moved into La Treille-Haute, her country house at Castelnaud, together with her mother and her son Riquet. Both women were staunch patriots, and both had a single end in view: they were eager to make as valuable a contribution to the Resistance as they could.

My first reaction on seeing Nandoue's lovely house was to marvel at the magnificent view it afforded of the Dordogne valley. The terrace overlooked the road from Castelnaud to Milandes, the railway line, and the whole of the plain below. No sooner had I inspected the property than I itched to move in there. Enclosed by a stout wall and shielded from prying eyes, the house would make a perfect little fortress. We would be able not only to detect the approach of any unwelcome visitors but to slip away through the woods with ease.

I had just arrived at this conclusion when Nandoue turned to me with a smile. 'Well, *Monsieur l'Anglais*, do you like the place? If so, it's yours.'

I could have kissed her. Thanks to Nandoue, I was going to enjoy the advantages of an ideal command post, at least for some time to come. A valuable bonus was that Malraux lived such a short distance away that we would be able to meet without difficulty.

I moved into La Treille the next day, accompanied by Jean-Pierre. Satisfied that we would never find a better spot for our radio transmissions, I also sent for Casimir, who promptly set up his aerial in the barn.

Some days later we were joined by my father and Dick the Alsatian, both of whom moved in with us. We remained at La Treille-Haute for several weeks. Nandoue's elderly mother, whom we came to love like our own flesh and blood, did

all she could to make our life pleasant, and young Riquet
seemed delighted to have some 'older boys' to play with.
Above all, though, there was Nandoue: caring, courageous,
and forever at pains to keep her visitors well fed and comfortably
housed. La Treille-Haute made an ideal hideout, but I couldn't
help worrying sometimes. What if the Germans turned up?
Concerned for Nandoue's safety, but also for Riquet and his
grandmother, I decided to look around for another base before
it was too late.

The Maquis

There is no point here in describing the organization of the
maquis or discussing the strategy and objectives of the Resistance.
Many others have done so already, some with total honesty,
others in a regrettably tendentious manner. I must, however,
devote some space to the Resistance forces in our area during
the two months prior to 6 June, 1944.

The Resistance forces in Dordogne and Corrèze fell into two
main groups: the Armée Secrète (AS) and the Francs-Tireurs
Partisans (FTP), the latter being communist-dominated.

The Dordogne AS was divided into three sectors whose
departmental chiefs were Gisèle (Commandant Boilet) and
Martial (Commandant Gaucher). The south-east sector was
commanded by Bergeret, who tended not to comply with
directives issued by the departmental authorities. This district
embraced a number of groups and local commanders: Pistolet
at Bergerac, Victor near Grolejac, Journier and Cerisier at
Lalinde, Albert at Sarlac, and so on. The central sector,
commanded by Roland (Clee), comprised several detachments
including, among others, Roland's own group, Marianne at
Vergt, Mercédès, and Bugeaud.

The northern sector, or Brigade Rac, was commanded by
Charles Serre, and, after his arrest, by Cezard.

The Dordogne FTP, who were organized along more
hierarchical lines, underwent some major changes in command.
Robert Delord was killed at Thenon, Jacky arrested at Limoges,
and André Bonnetot (Vincent), whom I have previously
mentioned, transferred to another post at the FTP's interregional

headquarters. They were replaced by Lecœur, Bernard, and Benjamin, who were later joined by Yves Peron (Caillou). Finally, Hercule de Terrasson joined the FTP's headquarters staff. The FTP were also divided into sectors like the Normand or Georges groups.

The MOI [*Mouvement Ouvrier International*, or International Labour Movement] consisted mainly of Spaniards and was commanded in Dordogne by Carlos. I admired Carlos and his men. They were true fighters, brave and self-disciplined, and I was on the best of terms with them and with Carlos himself.

In Corrèze, which was organized along the same lines, the AS maintained a sizeable maquis commanded by two regular army captains named Vaujour and Guédin, who developed it into a very effective fighting force on military lines. The Corrèze FTP were equally well organized and conducted some daring operations.

This very general account of the Dordogne and Corrèze maquis units may convey the impression that they had a strictly defined chain of command. In fact, as I have previously stated, the maquis commanders were very independent operators. The responsibility they felt for their men, whose daily fears and dangers, triumphs and disasters they shared, rendered them jealous of their prerogatives. They had learned to get by on their own and most of them had gained authority over their subordinates by personal example.

On returning from Paris I set off with Malraux/Berger (as I shall call him in Resistance contexts) on a veritable tour of the maquis. It was a risky undertaking, because we had to criss-cross wide expanses of Corrèze, Dordogne and Lot by car, using minor roads, and there was always the chance of an untoward encounter.

Our primary task was to gauge the potential of the units we visited as accurately as possible, estimate their arms requirements and, in certain cases, assess their need for weapons instructors. I talked these problems over with Malraux/Berger and the unit commanders, and we sometimes consented to arrange an air drop. The decision whether or not to make one was the outcome of delicate discussions with the maquis leaders. The Allies were sparing with their consignments of arms, so my choices were subject to very strict criteria.

I was at this time sending message after message to London asking the authorities to step up the frequency of their air drops. I don't know if my messages finally took effect, or if Allied policy subsequently changed, but I must concede that the service I received assumed adequate proportions later on. There is no doubt that the organization of eighty-plus arms drops was one of the Nestor/Digger network's most outstanding achievements.

Malraux/Berger's particular concern during these visits to the maquis was to foster a climate favourable to his future relations with them. He brought his experience and enthusiasm to bear on all who were leading a precarious existence in the wilds, and he often succeeded in creating a very good impression. At the outset of our tour, however, he sometimes ran into difficulties because the maquis commanders promptly realized that 'Colonel Berger' was none other than André Malraux.

This could prove a liability. Certain members of the AS took him for a communist, whereas the FTP distrusted him because he 'wasn't a communist any longer'. Although the AS authorities got over their misgivings more readily than the leaders of the FTP, the latter were practical men. A standard-bearer of Malraux's calibre was not to be sneezed at, and the air drops arranged by 'Captain Jack' were another factor worthy of consideration.

Irked none the less by the attitude of certain FTP commanders, Malraux/Berger made his famous two-handed gesture – the one that outlined an imaginary box.

'They're *curés,* my dear Jack, narrow-minded *curés,*' he said with a laugh. 'Better go and see them on your own. After all, they're friends of yours.'

He was exaggerating. However, my personal relations with the FTP were good for several reasons, the first being my excellent rapport with Vincent (Bonnetot) while at Brive with Henri Peulevé, the second my lack of ingrained prejudice against communists. I had shared a Spanish prison with communists, the Red Army was acquitting itself magnificently on the Eastern Front, and the maquisards of the FTP were brave men. I also possessed a friend in Charles the Bolshevik, and I was too young to have grasped the full implications of the Spanish Civil War or even of the German-Soviet Pact in 1939. My one, overriding idea was to co-operate wholeheartedly with all who were fighting the Nazis and their French confederates.

The communist authorities must have felt a certain liking for the peculiar Englishman known as Captain Jack, and their good will often simplified matters.

My personal relations with Malraux, though cordial, were not as much governed by boundless admiration as the uninformed reader might suppose.

At my age, I had only a sketchy knowledge of the pre-war Malraux. Mine was a new generation, one in whom circumstances had bred a certain justified mistrust of its elders. We blamed them for our country's lack of military preparedness. Moreover, the intensive course of technical, physical and psychological training I had undergone in England had left me less malleable than before. I was not, therefore, dominated by André Malraux, even though I recognized that he was a born leader and an exceptional personality. And, being very practical, I considered that my association with him would be beneficial to our common task, which was to rid our country of the enemy. The influence wielded by 'Colonel Berger' over other members of the SOE was less perceptible because some of them had known nothing about him when they arrived in France. The sole exceptions were my compatriot Gilbert (M. Gerschel, who landed by parachute in July, 1944) and, of course, George Hiller, who was operating in Lot.

The weeks preceding the Allied landing were exceedingly strenuous. I continued to criss-cross Dordogne and Corrèze by car, keeping to the minor roads. I would visit a maquis detachment or supervise one of my nocturnal air drops, then double back to La Treille-Haute to brief myself on the messages Casimir had received from London in my absence. I took part in attacks on the enemy and sabotage operations, often simply to show my face, because the presence of an Allied representative helped to sustain the Resistance idea in the minds of young maquisards fresh from their homes, friends, and villages.

The maquis formations were gaining strength. The Germans no longer ventured into rural areas except in substantial numbers. Although we risked running into them at road junctions and our camps came under attack, we could get around more easily than before as long as we avoided towns and large villages. Having lived in towns, where the threat of arrest was ever-present, I felt far safer driving through the countryside.

My participation in raids and acts of sabotage did not always go according to plan. One such occasion was the attack on the Thuillères dam.

Accompanied by Jean-Pierre, I had gone to inspect some maquis units under the command of Bergeret. During our visit the leader of the group disclosed that he was mounting an attack on the Thuillères dam that very night and suggested that we take part in the operation. We set off for the dam at nightfall and made our way across the wooded hills for several kilometres. Jean-Pierre and I were annoyed because we had failed to elicit any precise details of the plan of attack. At last, after a good hour's march, we were informed that we had reached the vicinity of the dam and must crawl the rest of the way. Being good at crawling, Jean-Pierre and I soon found ourselves up with the leaders. It was a dark night. Someone had just come to ask Jean-Pierre for a few tips on the use of the bazooka he had been issued when some powerful searchlights came on, dazzling us. The Germans had been expecting us and, before we knew what was happening, they opened up with machine guns. I was infuriated by such a deplorable lack of preparation.

Everyone fled. Jean-Pierre and I dived into the undergrowth and quickly reached some dead ground. We started laughing.

'You know the story of the parrot on the sinking ship?' I said.

'Sure,' said Jean-Pierre, 'it's a classic: "For a mug's game, this is a mug's game".'

But there were also some more successful operations: for instance a mission I entrusted to Carlos, the resolute and efficient commander of the Spanish maquis. I had every confidence in him and his Spaniards, who had spent years living under arduous conditions and were exceptionally well versed in sabotage and guerrilla warfare. Besides, Carlos was a *gran señor!*

I had asked Carlos to blow up a railway line regularly used by trains bound for Germany. Whether or not I explained my requirements in too much detail, he smiled and said, 'Why not come with us? Then we can see which technique is the better, British or Spanish Republican.'

I duly set out by night with Carlos and his maquisards. I wanted the track severed at two points fifty metres apart.

When we reached the first of them, Carlos simply said, '*À vous, señor.*' I laid my charge while he and his men looked on with a critical eye. When I had completed my preparations, I heard him say, 'Bravo, *muy bien!*' We walked on for another fifty metres, and I left Carlos to lay our second charge. Then we lit our respective fuses and hurriedly took cover. Night turned into day, and there were two enormous, almost simultaneous explosions. The other men headed back to base at once, but Carlos and I could not resist taking a look at the results of our handiwork. We made our way down the embankment in silence.

'That was quite a racket,' Carlos said eventually. 'Perhaps we'd better leave before someone pokes his nose in.'

I have already mentioned my reluctance to impose upon Nandoue for too long. In spite of all our efforts and, in particular, of the unremitting watch kept on all visitors to the house by my father, 'Commandant Robert', our hideout was becoming too well known. The risk of some breach of security was steadily increasing.

Although I had failed to agree with 'Soleil' on the formation of a reliable combat group capable of responding to London's specific requests in the field of sabotage and guerrilla warfare, Malraux/Berger had introduced me to a number of talented individuals who promised to be very useful to us. They included Colonel de Rochebouet, an intelligence expert; Captain Bernhardi, an Algerian-born Frenchman who had landed up in the Dordogne and wanted to take an active part in our operations; two courageous and enthusiastic young men named Lescot and Chateaurenaud; and, later on, Christian Plaçais, an efficient NCO from the Valmy group, a first-class outfit. It was Plaçais who, under Commandant Robert's supervision, was to recruit a combat unit capable of carrying out the missions I had originally meant to entrust to 'Soleil'.

Malraux/Berger and I agreed that the local situation was developing rapidly and that it was in our joint interests to keep in even closer touch from now on and live like maquisards, or almost! Bernhardi offered us the use of the Château de la Vitrolle at Limeuil. We would be safe there, and it was more comfortable than living under canvas.

129

So we said goodbye to Nandoue and her courageous family and moved into the château, a handsome house not far from the confluence of the Vézère and the Dordogne. The novel feature of this move was that we would all be living under the same roof: Malraux/Berger, his friends, the men of the combat unit, Commandant Robert, Jean-Pierre, and my radio operator, Casimir. The Limeuil set-up was an efficient one. We had everyone within easy reach plus two channels of telephonic communication upstream and downstream of the château. These were provided by the postmistresses of Limeuil, Le Bugue, Tremolat, and Lalinde. It was, of course, the job of those ladies to warn us at once if any suspicious visitors showed up.

I don't know who first thought of giving our team its name. Could some visitor have asked the sentries on guard duty if he was at inter-allied headquarters? Was it Malraux/Berger's doing? Whatever the truth, it was not long before the entire regional Resistance movement began to refer to us as Inter-Allied Headquarters. It wasn't a bad idea – we were allies, after all, and we were a Franco-British outfit. This term had a catalysing effect on the whole of the local maquis. I was the only person able to secure regular contact with the Allies in London, so why shouldn't we call ourselves Inter-Allied Headquarters or Inter-Allied Command Post? All else apart, we really did operate under the orders of COSSAC, chief of staff to General Eisenhower, the Supreme Allied Commander.

On the Eve of D-Day

The development of the Resistance had clarified itself. The maquis had definitely taken over in small groups and in built-up areas.

There still were some *résistants* in the towns, it is true, but most of them had become incorporated in the various regional maquis formations. We were taking on recruits. More and more young men, unwilling to be conscripted into the STO* and

---

**Service du Travail Obligatoire*, the Compulsory Labour Service set up by Vichy under German pressure.

sent off to Germany, were joining our ranks. Many of our more hesitant brethren had finally decided to cross the Rubicon. We were beginning to encounter the odd regular officer who had also joined us for various reasons. The eve of D-Day witnessed a rapid growth in the size of the Resistance. The maquis units were becoming operational and occupying whole tracts of countryside. Perturbed by this development, the Germans kept to the towns, though they sometimes undertook punitive expeditions that proved extremely costly to both sides. The men of the maquis were fast becoming adept at guerrilla warfare, and it was not long before they began to inflict heavy losses on the Germans.

Under these new circumstances, Limeuil and the Château de la Vitrolle made it possible for us to control the whole team from a central location. At the same time, these very advantages rendered us vulnerable to denunciation and sudden attack.

Communal life enabled us to get to know each other better, and there were evenings when conversation became lively. I recall one such occasion.

'The Resistance is changing fast,' someone said. 'We're going to be gobbled up by the *naphthalinés*.* They'll outnumber us before long, and then they'll start teaching us our own business!'

'Don't be too hard on the newcomers,' said someone else. 'Up to now the Resistance wouldn't have known what to do with large numbers of recruits. We had to be small to be leakproof and effective, but things have changed. Let them all come – the more the merrier. It won't be long before we're fighting out in the open.'

'I think the French have been hoodwinked by Pétain and Vichy,' I said, 'or most of them, at least. The fence-sitters couldn't bring themselves to admit that Pétain is a pernicious individual. They've failed to see, throughout these years, that the honour of France transcends all Vichy's ploys and double-dealing, and that de Gaulle personifies it. They're beginning to realize that now, and so much the better.'

---

*'The mothballed ones', i.e. those who had hitherto kept their heads down and steered clear of the Resistance.

Berger/Malraux, who had been listening intently, seemed surprised to hear a 'British' officer give vent to such sentiments. He thought hard, then launched into a long dissertation of his own. It featured Pontius Pilate, the original Marathon runner, Alexander the Great, and, of course, Lawrence of Arabia. What really mattered, as he saw it, was to discover the true extent of de Gaulle's stature and intelligence.

'I don't know him and I don't like his speeches,' he said, 'but if he makes his mark with the Allies we'll have won the war. If not,' and here he made a sweeping gesture, 'go and see your friends in the FTP!'

VII
D-DAY AND AFTER

Les maquis de l'A.S.-M.U.R.-Corrèze
immobilisent pendant plusieurs jours la DAS-REICH, meilleure division blindée S. S. d'HITLER

(Journal de marche du 5 juin au 22 août 1944)

5 JUIN 1944

Les messages ordonnant les coupures de routes, voies ferrées et de guérillas passent à la radio.

6 JUIN 1944

1 — *Départ du camp de CAMPS à 14 heures; la Brigade, aux ordres des capitaines HERVE et GEORGES, comprend :*

Le bataillon « maquis » aux ordres du capitaine ROMAIN (1er bataillon).

1re compagnie : lieutenant REMY.
2e compagnie : lieutenant GILBERT.
3e compagnie : lieutenant DESTRE.
La compagnie « maquis » BARTHES.

La compagnie « maquis » Nord-Africaine : lieutenant COULON.

Le bataillon « maquis » aux ordres du capitaine PIERRE, secondé par les capitaines GUIBERT, PIERROT et LE BRETON, qui se forme aux environs de POMPADOUR et de TERRASSON.

Le groupement DURET, qui se forme aux environs d'USSEL.

Le groupement HUBERT, qui se forme aux environs de TULLE.

Les trois compagnies civiles de BRIVE, aux ordres des lieutenants LASSALLE, THOMAS, CHAMPTIAUX, THEILLOT et GAO.

2 — *Le P.C. de la brigade est établi à SAINTE-FEREOLE et le dispositif est mis en place :*

a) Sur les ponts de la Dordogne S'EYLAC à GROSLEJAC.
b) Sur les axes TOULOUSE-LIMOGES à CRESSENSSAC et NOAILLES.

FIGEAC - MONTARGIS à BRETENOUX et LA GRAFOUILLIERE.

c) Des postes à NOAILLES, RIAUME et LANTEUIL protègent le dispositif.

18 heures : *Accrochage de la 1re compagnie à SOUILLAC avec un poste de guet allemand. Allemands : 7 hommes certainement tués, dont 4 officiers, 2 camions détruits ainsi qu'une V.L. et 1 moto.*

Français : 3 blessés, 1 commotionné.

Vers 20 heures 30 : Accrochage de la 1re compagnie contre un train blindé stationnant à SOUILLAC.

Allemands : 7 tués.

Nous n'avons pas de pertes. Pendant ce temps, l'A.S., civile du LOT, en liaison avec la

2e compagnie, attaque un train de ravitaillement sur la ligne d'AURILLAC.

Allemands : 2 tués, 13 prisonniers.

Français : 1 tué.

7 JUIN 1944

Le P.C. est établi dans la source à LA GRAFOUILLIERE. La compagnie BARTHES arrête un train blindé à NOAILLES.

Colonel René VAUJOUR

ALIAS « HERVE »
ET « PATRICK »

Chef départemental de l'A. S. - M. U. R. Corrèze

Allemands : 16 hommes hors de combat.

Français : 3 tués.

Dans l'après-midi, la 1re compagnie attaque au pont de SOUILLAC une colonne avant-garde de la division blindée « Das Reich », immobilisant 1 V. L. et 5 camions.

Allemands : pertes inconnues.

Français : 1 tué.

Mort des suites de blessures.

La 3e compagnie capture, en gare de VAYRAC, 7 Allemands qui appartenaient au train de ravitaillement attaqué le 6 juin.

8 JUIN 1944

Vers 16 heures, la P.C. du bataillon attaque de front les éléments de tête de la division « Das Reich » à CRESSENSSAC. Le combat dure 3 heures.

Les Allemands subissent des pertes élevées et passent après avoir débordé la résistance. Nous avons 5 tués, 3 blessés et 10 disparus. Dans la nuit, une embuscade tendue au nord de CRESSENSSAC cause de nouvelles pertes dans les colonnes allemandes.

Au pont de GROSLEJAC, la 1re compagnie immobilise une A. M. et tue 6 Allemands.

Nous avons 1 tué.

A ROUFFILLAC, la 1re compagnie attaque une colonne blindée, détruisant 1 moto, 2 A. M. : 1 camion, endommageant 1 char léger.

Allemands : 52 tués 64 blessés (d'après un officier allemand).

Français : 1 tué, 2 blessés.

9 JUIN 1944

Dans la matinée, vers 6 heures 30, le pont de Brete-nous, tenu par la 3e compagnie, est attaqué d'abord par des éléments d'infanterie de la division « Das Reich » qui ne réussissent pas à passer, puis par des blindés qui tentent le passage à 10 heures 30. Les Allemands éprouvent de lourdes pertes et nous avons 17 tués et 2 blessés.

Le bouchon de BEAULIEU saute à 10 heures 30. Nous avons 1 tué.

A 12 heures, le poste de GRAFOUILLIERE est débordé. Nous avons 1 tué.

L'action des unités de la brigade contre le Panzer « Das Reich » a infligé un retard de 48 heures à cette unité et a permis ainsi à la R.A.F. de l'attaquer près d'ANGOULEME et de lui causer de lourdes pertes.

10 AU 16 JUIN 1944

Le P.C. s'installe au ROC-BLANC-NESTEVE. — Réorganisation des unités engagées, formation de nouvelles unités armées montées au camp d'instruction, 6e et 7e Cies).

17 JUIN 1944

Une section de la 2e compagnie, installée en embuscade sur la R. N. 20, au sud du LANZAC, attaque une colonne descendant vers le sud : 1 V.L. détruite, 7 tués, 10 blessés du côté allemand. Nous avons 3 blessés légers.

18 JUIN 1944

La 2e compagnie, une embuscade sur la R.N. 20, au sud du LANZAC, tient en échec pendant 3 heures un convoi de 90 camions.

Allemands : 40 tués, dont 7 officiers, 65 blessés, 2 camions brûlés, 1 tourelle hors d'état, 1 A.M. en remorque.

Français : aucune perte.

19 JUIN 1944

Une section de la 2e compagnie, en embuscade sur la R.N. 20 au sud du LANZAC, attaque une colonne allemande motorisée, détruisant 1 side, 1 V.L., 2 camions, 1 remorque blindée, tuant 32 Allemands, dont 3 officiers, en blessant 40. Les Allemands fuient dans les bois. Nous n'avons pas de pertes.

25 JUIN 1944

La 1re compagnie attaque une patrouille motorisée allemande près de SALIGNAC : 5 V.L. hors d'usage, 30 tués, 6 blessés. Pas de pertes françaises.

Général GUEDIN

alias colonel « GEORGES »

Chef des 7.000 Maquisards de l'A.S.-M.U.R. Corrèze

26 ET 27 JUIN 1944

Après avoir échappé à deux manœuvres d'encerclement au sud de SOUILLAC, une section de la 2e compagnie attaque le 27, au PAS-DE-RAYSSE un détachement motorisé immobilisé : 1 V.L. détruite, 7 tués 10 blessés du côté allemand.

Allemands : 17 tués dont 2 officiers, 25 blessés, 4 véhicules dont 2 camions.

Français : pas de pertes.

6 ET 7 JUILLET 1944

La section WIARD, du P.C. du 1er bataillon, bloque sous

un tunnel près de GIGNAC, sur la voie ferrée BRIVE-SOUILLAC, un train de voyageurs, arrêtant ainsi pour de nombreux jours le trafic sur une des deux voies.

8 JUILLET 1944

La compagnie LECOCQ, du groupement DURET, tend une embuscade dans les gorges du CHAVANNON.

Allemands : 25 tués, dont l'officier commandant la compagnie d'USSEL, 2 prisonniers.

Français : aucune perte.

14 JUILLET 1944

Un parachutage important d'armes permet de transformer l'ordre de bataille de la brigade.

Le bataillon ROMAIN (ci-le 1er bataillon de Cœur), BARTHES est intégrée dans le 2e bataillon, commandé par le commandant GERMAIN (As de Pique).

La compagnie NORD-AFRICAINE s'équipant et de jeunes éléments provenant du camp (compagnie ROBERT), devient le 3e bataillon commandé par le capitaine CHEVALLIER (As de Carreau).

Le bataillon PIERRE devient le bataillon As de trèfle).

Les groupements DURET et HUBERT, augmentant rapidement leurs effectifs et atteignent chacun la valeur de 3 bataillons. Le groupement DURET prend le nom de demi-brigade de Haute-Corrèze et le groupement HUBERT celui de groupe franc de Tulle.

19 JUILLET 1944

La section du commandant GUEDIN qui depuis le 8 juin n'avait pas cessé d'entretenir les coupures sur la voie ferrée SOUILLAC-BRIVE est prise à partie par un train blindé; après un combat d'une heure, la destruction prévue est opérée.

Pertes allemandes inconnues. Nous avons 2 blessés et 1 laissons 2 prisonniers.

22 JUILLET 1944

La compagnie LECOCQ, de la demi-brigade de Haute-Corrèze, sur la R.N. 89, attaque un camion près de SAINT-DEZERY.

Allemands : 2 tués et 6 blessés.

Français : 2 tués.

Suite page 12

The maquis of the Corrèze AS-MUR [Secret Army-United Resistance Movement] keep the 'Das Reich', the best armoured division in Hitler's SS, pinned down for several days.

D-Day

The weeks preceding the Normandy invasion were a trying time. Although we had absolute faith in final victory, we could not but feel extremely apprehensive in the meantime. If the Allied landing were delayed and the Germans attacked us in strength, it was doubtful how long we could hold off an army as efficient as the enemy's.

Although the Resistance was steadily growing in numbers, young and inexperienced recruits were a questionable asset. They presented the maquis commanders with almost insoluble problems of security and supervision.

My efforts in the sphere of air drops had definitely paid off, but our needs were assuming critical proportions. I bombarded the SOE with messages requesting arms, but the response was always the same: it was impossible to step up supplies without penalizing more exposed areas once the landing had taken place. When I stressed the large numbers of young men now joining the maquis, I received a reply that infuriated me: London suggested sending them home!

'They're crazy,' I told Casimir and Jean-Pierre. 'Do they honestly think I can go to the maquis commanders and tell them to send their boys home?'

'Be careful,' London instructed me. 'Form small, well-trained guerrilla groups. Avoid large concentrations.'

This was manifestly sound advice. I agreed with it where security and strategic mobility were concerned, but its implementation on the ground was not always feasible. Many local commanders preferred to exercise close control over their men rather than see them disperse into the countryside in small groups, so a certain amount of incomprehension reigned between us and our bosses on the other side of the Channel.

I was having more and more difficulty in allaying the impatience of Malraux/Berger and the leaders of the maquis. They knew that I was doing my utmost, but they were becoming more and more afraid that a major German offensive would catch them empty-handed. Meanwhile, London continued to treat us to the hot-and-cold-shower régime.

On 15 May I received a very laconic message requesting me to find some sites suitable for the landing of a substantial number of airborne troops. I duly reconnoitred these sites. Was it the landing proper, I wondered, or just a diversion? It would be our job to secure the sites while the operation was in progress, so I was obliged to confer with one or two local commanders. It took only forty-eight hours for the word to get around, as I discovered when some comrades of mine came to tell me that the Allies were going to land in Dordogne.

London approved the sites I suggested. A few days later I was informed that the air drop would involve a mere dozen men who were to place themselves at my disposal. This operation was subsequently cancelled, or at least postponed until July.

London also proposed to send me a courier, a second-in-command, and so forth. I already had plenty of splendid couriers in Dordogne and Corrèze – Flora, Madeleine and Georgette, to name only three – so there was no need to land any girls by parachute. As for a second-in-command, Jean-Pierre [Peter Lake], the instructor sent me by London, had proved to be a first-class lieutenant.

'No thanks,' I radioed back. 'All we need is arms.'

And, to be honest, we did receive a substantial number of air drops during the latter half of May.

I was spending the evening of 1 June with Malraux/Berger, Colonel Robert, De Rochebouet and one or two others when Casimir entered the château's drawing-room. With an obvious air of excitement, he asked me to accompany him to the room where his transmitter was installed. As soon as we were outside he handed me a slip of paper.

'I had a tough job decoding this,' he said. 'It was double-enciphered. Read it.'

'Important message for Nestor *stop*,' I read. 'Major operation scheduled in the next few days *stop* You will be notified by the BBC twenty-four hours before operations commence *stop* The relevant message will be "The giraffe has a long neck" *stop* Your task will be to sabotage railway lines, destroy petrol dumps, and maximize disruption to the enemy's lines of communication *stop* Execute well-timed guerrilla operations but avoid any large-scale action that could expose the civilian population to reprisals.'

I thought at once of the landing, but I remained circumspect. After all, it was barely two weeks since we had burned our fingers on the airborne operation that was ultimately cancelled. My first task was to alert the Resistance authorities. They had to prepare for action without arousing an excess of enthusiasm that might trigger dangerous commotions or indiscretions.

I rejoined the others and informed them that I had just received a message from London which seemed to indicate that a large-scale operation would be launched in the next few days.

'It's the landing!' Malraux/Berger exclaimed.

'It could be,' I said cautiously. 'We must inform the maquis commanders but ensure that they don't jump the gun. We must be prepared in any case. The landing can't be much longer.'

I didn't mention the BBC's coded message. 'The giraffe' remained a secret between me and Casimir.

Casimir and I shut ourselves up in the radio room every evening and listened to the personal messages. '*Ici Londres. Les Français parlent aux Français!*' We were huddled over the set on the night of 4 June when, all at once, I heard:

'Important message for Nestor: "The giraffe has a long neck."'

I jumped up and flung my arms around Casimir. So many years of waiting, so many hopes and disappointments, so much suffering, but now – by God! – the time had come. Unable to contain my delight, I summoned the others.

'Robert, Poulou, Bernhardi, de Rochebouet, Michel, Jean-Pierre, Christian! This is it, gentlemen! The landing is imminent!'

Malraux/Berger was away, but I had to inform him too. I set off by car with Jean-Pierre and Poulou to alert the maquis commanders. I shall never forget that headlong drive through the night. I finally found 'Colonel Berger' with a maquis detachment in Dordogne.

'It's tomorrow!' I cried.

The hour of the Resistance had struck. It was time to harass, ambush, sabotage – to do all in our power to disrupt the enemy's operations.

Between the receipt of my message and the morrow of the official news of the landing, maquis units of the FFI [French Forces of the Interior] launched a series of major operations. Railway lines of vital importance to the enemy were sabotaged with outstanding success. The twin tracks of two arterial routes, Bordeaux-Périgueux-Brive and Limoges-Périgueux-Agen, were subjected to attack by the maquis (often ably assisted by railwaymen). The Thiviers-Angoulême and, in Dordogne, Périgueux-Agen lines were also sabotaged, and numerous dumps of valuable enemy equipment were destroyed. On the roads, maquisards took effective control of the situation by setting up road-blocks at certain key points. I myself participated in these sabotage operations, but it was Jean-Pierre who really went to town in the east of Dordogne.

The news of D-Day generated an incredible climate of enthusiasm within a few hours, but it also gave rise to some anxiety. Although most members of the Resistance kept their heads, some were so carried away by events that they became inordinately euphoric. We were genuinely alarmed, for example, to learn that Bergeret (Loupias) had proclaimed the Fourth Republic and appointed himself prefect at Bergerac, where French flags were flying from every window. German troops were only a few kilometres away. If they stepped in, as they might within hours, there was every chance that a bloodbath would result. All the makings of a tragedy were present, as we could clearly see.

Malraux/Berger and I at once conferred with Martial and Gisèle, who headed the AS in Dordogne, and implored them to reason with the over-excited persons concerned. Being in full agreement with us, they acted promptly.

What made the situation still more explosive was that hundreds of young and not-so-young men had taken to the roads of Corrèze and Dordogne on their way to join the maquis, and the arrival of all these volunteers presented grave security problems.

I had been alarmed enough during April and May by the large concentrations of men joining the maquis, but this was nothing compared to the phenomenon we were now witnessing. Most of the maquis commanders reacted sensibly and dispersed their new recruits in the countryside. Others, unfortunately, regarded the influx as an opportunity to swell their ranks.

Under these circumstances, shortages of arms and equipment were bound to make themselves felt more than ever. Unit commanders were also confronted by serious logistical problems, e.g. how to feed and house youngsters unaccustomed to roughing it in the woods.

Reviewing the events immediately following D-Day, one has to conclude that, although some degree of chaos and indiscipline reigned, Resistance operations were generally effective. Alarmed by this upheaval, the Germans were temporarily outflanked and deterred from leaving the towns where they maintained garrisons. We were none the less aware of the dangers that still threatened. If the Allies secured a foothold in Normandy, the German high command would summon reinforcements, and certain crack troops stationed near Montauban, further to the south-west, would logically have to pass us on their way to the Normandy front.

Moreover, I had received a message from London to the effect that, if German troops traversed our area, we must do our utmost to slow them down by laying ambushes and sabotaging their lines of communication. At the same time, we were to avoid a general uprising that might imperil the local inhabitants.

The 'Das Reich' Division

The German response was not long in coming. On 10 June the curfew was reinstituted. The tricolour flags were temporarily put away. The Germans organized punitive expeditions, but they encountered stiff resistance on the part of the maquis.

On the morning of 8 June an immense column of tanks and armoured cars set off from a point near Montauban and headed towards us on its way to the Normandy front.

Several books have been written about the 'Das Reich' Division's actions in the course of its journey to Normandy.

For example, no one will ever forget the massacre at Oradour-sur-Glane.

Some writers have belittled the Resistance operations against the 'Das Reich'. I think they fail to grasp the environment and circumstances in which the men of the maquis had to wage their unequal struggle against an élite armoured division.

Their objective was to delay the 'Das Reich' for as long as possible by means of hit-and-run tactics and acts of sabotage. They were irregulars, not an army in the field. How could we have expected them, brave and resolute though they were, to destroy or substantially diminish the fire-power of one of Hitler's best divisions? The Resistance attained its objective. It put up an admirable fight and succeeded in delaying the division by several days.

This is not a figment of my imagination. When the war ended I was received by the British minister of economic warfare, a member of Churchill's war cabinet. He told me in the presence of witnesses that General Eisenhower estimated that Resistance attacks on the 'Das Reich' had delayed its arrival at the front by at least a week.

The division underwent countless attacks by our maquis units, which operated for the most part in small detachments. Jean-Pierre (Peter Lake) and three comrades blew up the track ahead of an armoured train carrying elements of the 'Das Reich'. The Germans halted to repair the track and steamed on, only to find, a few kilometres down the line, that Jean-Pierre had been there before them. The result: yet another hold-up. All maquis units were mobilized to take part in this delaying action. It is true that the Germans themselves contributed to the delay by ferociously and foolishly pursuing the maquisards into villages and the open countryside instead of pressing on as fast as possible. The fact remains that they got to Normandy later than they would have done otherwise, and that their morale was not, perhaps, as high as it had been.

The northward advance of the 'Das Reich' subjected the maquisards to an enormous strain, but they acquitted themselves with courage and determination. They can justly pride themselves on having made a substantial contribution to the Allied cause at this decisive stage of the war.

Prelude to the Liberation

But the fight went on. Germans were still in our area, and we had to move out of Limeuil.

I had just returned from a mission with Jean-Pierre when the telephone in the hallway of the Château de la Vitrolle rang. Paul Lachaud, who answered it, recognized the caller's voice at once. It was the postmistress at Lalinde.

'Good evening,' she said calmly. 'Some tanks are on the way.'

There was no possibility of fighting off tanks with our handful of machine guns, so I instructed Robert to assemble everything and everyone and get Casimir and his radio to a place of safety. I got the impression that my father had performed this operation several times before, because it took him only a few minutes to make the arrangements and stow everything in two small trucks and a car, ready to move out.

Émile Chateaurenaud, a new recruit and a courageous and likeable young man, volunteered to go and see what the Germans were up to. Setting off on his motorbike, he came face to face with the enemy less than a kilometre from the château. They opened fire without more ado, and that day, 23 June, 1944, we lost a valuable young *résistant*.

Robert and his little convoy moved off. I decided to go and make sure that none of Casimir's radio equipment had been left behind. Poulou kept watch while I quickly climbed to Casimir's base of operations at the top of the house. I was on my way down again when I heard him call, 'Quick, the Boches are coming!'

I ran to the château's garden gate and saw the tanks about to drive in. There was only one thing for it, and that was to make for the river, which was fifty metres away.

'Run for it, Poulou!' I shouted.

A machine gun opened up. They had spotted us. The river seemed a very long way off. We were about to dive in when we were hailed by a man peacefully fishing from a dinghy near the bank.

'Having trouble?' he inquired, deadpan. 'If so, hop in.'

Well screened by the trees on the bank we had just left, we got across the river unscathed.

Français !

Il y avait dans le département de la Dordogne, un village tranquille et paisible : **Mouleydier.**
Depuis toujours une population laborieuse y vivait dans le calme à ses occupations.

Mais voici que vint le maquis !

Dans toutes les maisons furent entreposées des réserves d'armes et de munitions. Les plus jeunes hommes furent mobilisés et les plus âgés affectés au service des renseignements. Quant aux femmes, elles furent envoyées dans les localités voisines pour y faire de l'espionnage.

Il n'y eut plus de maire pour veiller au maintien de la justice et de l'ordre : le commandement fut assumé au village par un bandit des anciennes brigades internationales d'Espagne, auteur de huit meurtres.

Les habitants reçurent 150 grammes de pain par jour, mais les « Chefs » disposaient d'une attribution triple. — Les assassinats et les vols des bandits étrangers troublaient tout le voisinage.

Alors l'armée allemande intervint.

Dès l'approche des soldats allemands, les lâches bandes de maquisards s'empressèrent de fuir en abandonnant la population sans défense.

Mais au cours du tir effectué contre le maquis, des réserves de munitions entreposées dans la localité par les terroristes explosèrent, mettant ainsi le feu à Mouleydier.

C'est ainsi qu'un village tout entier fut détruit.
Fallait-il vraiment en arriver là ?

Si la population de Mouleydier avait — comme elle le fit tardivement — attiré tout de suite l'attention des autorités françaises ou allemandes sur la présence dans les environs d'un camp de bandits, tous ces maux lui auraient été épargnés.

FRANÇAIS, pensez toujours à cela ! Si des maquisards ou des agents étrangers apparaissent dans votre région, avant que les bandes s'installent, avertissez-en immédiatement les autorités les plus proches.....

...et vous sauverez ainsi vos maisons, vos fermes et vos vies !

S W 33 a

Frenchmen!

In the department of Dordogne there used to be a tranquil, peaceful village: **Mouleydier.**

The inhabitants had quietly gone about their business since time immemorial.

But then came the Maquis!

Stocks of arms and ammunition were stored in all the houses. The youngest men were mobilized and the eldest recruited into the intelligence service. As for the womenfolk, they were sent out to spy in neighbouring villages.

There was no mayor left to supervise the maintenance of justice and order: command of the village was assumed by a bandit from the former International Brigades of Spain, the perpetrator of eight murders. The inhabitants received 150 grams of bread a day, but the 'bosses' got a threefold allocation. The whole neighbourhood was plagued by the foreign bandits' murders and thefts.

Then the German Army stepped in.

The cowardly gangs of maquisards hurriedly fled at the approach of German soldiers, leaving the population defenceless.

While the Maquis were being shot at, however, stocks of ammunition stored in the village by the terrorists exploded, setting fire to Mouleydier.

That was how an entire village was destroyed. Did it really have to come to that?

If the inhabitants of Mouleydier had immediately drawn the French or German authorities' attention to the presence of a bandit camp in the vicinity, as they belatedly did, all these misfortunes would have been avoided.

Frenchmen, always bear that in mind! If maquisards or foreign agents appear in your district, promptly inform the nearest authorities before such gangs settle in . . .

. . . and you will save your houses, your farms, and your lives!

Dear Fisherman, many thanks. I never saw you again and have no idea who you were, but I shall never forget you.

Charles (Robert Brouillet) had no difficulty in finding us some new quarters in the Château de la Poujade at Urval, near Siorac. This château belonged to the Marquis de Commarque, a brave man whom the Germans had arrested and shot in 1942. The Marquise de Commarque, who was British by origin, willingly entrusted us with her house. She did not live there, but she came to see us while we were settling in.

'I leave the place in your care,' she told me, and added, in a discreet undertone, 'There are a few decent bottles left in the cellar. Try to keep them safe for me.'

I did my best, but, to my great shame, a few went missing at the time of the Liberation. (Years later, when I saw the Commarque family again, I learned that I had been forgiven.)

Not for the first time, Georgette proved a tower of strength. She not only coped with all our food-supply problems but, when necessary, did the cooking herself.

The chateau was perched on a wooded hill from which we could easily keep the road from the valley under observation. Strategically speaking, it was a first-class defensive position, not that we ever had to use it as such.

One afternoon we were informed that a German convoy escorted by an armoured car was coming along the road from Siorac. This time I decided to stand and fight if it came to the château. We watched the Germans' approach from a window. Sure enough, they turned off along the little road from Urval, in other words, the road to the château. We were ready for them within a couple of minutes. Jean-Pierre, Christian Plaçais and I concealed some well-armed men in the ditches beside the road and Jean-Pierre manned our bazooka. I explained that we would attack only if the Germans entered the grounds of the château, and that no one was to open fire unless or until I gave the signal. It was pointless to take risks that might have disastrous repercussions on the inhabitants of Urval and Siorac.

I have never understood what went on in the mind of the German officer in command of that convoy. The vehicles came within about two hundred metres of our hidden position. Then, the road being wider at that point, they abruptly turned and drove off. Had they lost their way? Were they scared? I shall never know.

Our activities intensified. Air drops had resumed in a satisfactory manner. One day, while touring a remote area with Malraux, I was surprised to see some youthful maquisards haring along the road towards us. I stopped the little red Simca I was driving and asked what was up.

'Tanks – German tanks,' they shouted. 'They're coming!'

I turned to Malraux. 'I wonder,' I said.

'So do I,' he replied. 'They're inexperienced youngsters, I'm sure they're exaggerating. Let's go and see.'

I drove on slowly for five minutes or so. There was nothing untoward to be seen, so I began to speed up. We rounded a corner rather fast, and there, only a stone's throw away, we came upon the German tanks. They were parked in echelon, and some of the crews had got out. The men must have been startled to see our little Simca bearing down on them.

I made the fastest skid-turn of my life. Malraux, who had climbed into the back, was firing at the enemy tanks with his popgun of a 7/65 revolver. I couldn't help laughing.

'You won't do much damage with that, André!'

My laughter quickly subsided. The Germans had recovered from their surprise and were firing back, but we got away without difficulty.

The episode at the Château de la Vitrolle had alerted me to the danger of having Casimir, our radio operator, constantly on the premises with us. The ideal solution, I thought, would be to find a place near the Château de la Poujade but outside its grounds. Charles, who came to my aid once more, suggested the house of an elderly film-maker who lived not far away.

'He's not in the Resistance,' he told me, 'but he's all right. His name is Léon Poirier.'

Commandant Robert and I glanced at each other in amusement. Léon Poirier was a cousin of ours. My father had known him well when young but had since lost touch; as for me, I didn't know him at all. A well-known director and a very orthodox Catholic, Léon had made an excellent film of the life of Père de Foucauld, which I had seen and been much impressed by before the war. He was also noted for having participated in the scientific expeditions in Africa and Central Asia sponsored by André Citroën. I asked Charles if he would be willing to put Casimir up.

'No idea,' he replied.

'We'd better pay him a visit,' said Robert.

Malraux looked dubious. 'I know the man,' he said. 'I've a feeling he was a Pétainist in 1940.'

All I gathered, in fact, was that he and Léon had clashed over some minor issue, Léon being such a devout Catholic, so Commandant Robert and I set off to call on our cousin.

Once inside his charming house at Urval, we introduced ourselves as neighbours paying a courtesy call. While these brief civilities were in progress I recognized Léon as a Poirier mainly by his eyes. He inspired total confidence. Clearly unconvinced by our story, Léon soon asked us what we really wanted.

'Very well,' I said. 'I'm an Allied officer who has been parachuted into this area to help the Resistance. I have with me another British officer, a radio operator. It's imperative that he transmit our messages to London from somewhere absolutely secure. Your house is the ideal place. Would you be willing to put him up?'

I and my father – pardon me, Commandant Robert – waited patiently. At last Léon broke the silence.

'What will happen to me and my wife if we agree and he's picked up by the Germans?'

'You'll both be shot,' I replied.

'Does he speak French, at least?'

'Yes,' said Commandant Robert, 'but badly.'

Léon gave me such a long look that I began to wonder if he had some inkling of our relationship. (He hadn't even recognized Robert, his first cousin.)

'Do I have any choice?' he asked at length.

I didn't reply.

'Very well,' he said, 'I agree. But I'm a film-maker, as you know, so I'm going to prepare a scenario for the benefit of our servants and friends. Your Englishman mustn't come here for another two days. During that time I shall announce that I'm expecting a cousin from Bordeaux who's going to spend some time with us. When he arrives he must fling his arms around my neck, kiss me on both cheeks, and address me as Léon, is that clear? Oh yes, and he mustn't talk too much.'

I burst out laughing. 'You've no need to worry on that score, *cher monsieur.*'

Léon Poirier, who did not discover that he was related to Commandant Robert and Captain Jack until after the Liberation, was very helpful to us in other ways. He lent us a small house situated behind his own. This was a perfect arrangement, so 'Inter-Allied Headquarters' continued to be based at La Poujade. To avoid unpleasant surprises when we were down in Urval at night, Malraux, Robert, Jean-Pierre and I used to sleep at Léon's cottage. He became more and more involved with the Resistance – so much so that he eventually volunteered his own property as a landing site. It was Léon himself, assisted by Poulou, Robert and Charles, who directed this air drop, which landed some containers almost inside his garden wall.

Things were too good to last. I began to have demarcation problems. I discovered that an SOE network whose operations I had thought confined to Lot-et-Garonne also maintained an outstation that encroached on my territory. Having first got wind of this in May, 1944, I became aware that the said network, which was doubtless engaged in a 'marketing' operation, had tried to make trouble for me: London had been informed by them that someone called Jack, with André Malraux in tow, was trying to impose his authority on all the local Resistance leaders. Their message, though sibylline, smacked strongly of a stab in the back. Infuriated by this development, I told London sharply that of course I was the 'Jack' in question, and that they knew perfectly well that Malraux and I were working together. I further stated that I was in touch with all the Resistance leaders within my allotted ambit and that I had never exceeded my authority. My message was understood and I heard no more of the affair. When we were at La Poujade some weeks later, however, I was told that someone called Edgar was in the Belves area and had been telling the Resistance authorities that he was the Allies' sole regional representative.

Anxious to get things sorted out at once, I asked my man Michel (Lucien Gambelon) to go and kidnap Edgar for me, which he expertly did. Edgar was blindfolded and brought to me at La Poujade. While conceding that this course of action may not have been 'cricket', I can claim that it was thoroughly effective. Under interrogation, Edgar told me that he worked for the SOE, that his code-name was Nero, that he belonged to the Hilaire network, and that his chief was Philibert. I went off to see Casimir, intending to check his statements with London, but Casimir was already in receipt of a message from London informing me that I had just shanghaied one of Hilaire's lieutenants, and that the situation was absolutely intolerable. Everything turned out all right, however, because London, having been told my reasons, instructed Edgar, Philibert and Hilaire to stop interfering in my area. I received the following signal, which ended the matter once and for all:

'86 *stop* Is Nero still with you? *stop* If so, pass him following message: *stop* "Order you report at once to Philibert if in contact with him *stop* If not direct to Hilaire *stop*."'

In clear, this meant that Nero was to desist from treading on my toes forthwith.

To banish any possible misunderstanding, I must record that the code-name Hilaire belonged to a British SOE officer named George Starr, who did an outstandingly good job in the south-west. His lieutenant, Philibert, was in fact Philippe de Gunzbourg, an aristocratic member of the Resistance. Nero was one of Philibert's lieutenants. I cherish the greatest respect for Philibert and Hilaire, and have recounted this incident only to illustrate the sort of problems we could encounter in the field, quite apart from any difficulties we may have had with the Resistance and the Germans. I would add that it was difficult at times to keep strictly within one's own territory. I myself was called to order for encroaching on the maquisards of Haute-Vienne and Creuse.

I have already described how I became an SOE agent, and how I did not learn until I reached London that General de Gaulle had set up an intelligence service of his own, the BCRA [see footnote on p. 87]. I also learned that rivalries existed between the two services, but I never became embroiled in them. It is not impossible that the BCRA maintained representatives in the areas where I was operating, but I neither met them nor heard them mentioned by the maquis. I concluded that the mission of a BCRA agent must be very different from my own.

On 16 June, 1944, I received a signal from London informing me that General Koenig had been appointed commander-in-chief of all the French Forces of the Interior (FFI), and that, accordingly, I would be under his command from now on. The message went on:

'General Koenig addresses the following directive to all military delegates currently operating, and you yourself must take this directive as an order *stop* Owing to the importance of the air operations in progress at the front, the arming of the Resistance will be a lengthy operation and must be integrated into a well-defined programme within the framework of military priorities *stop* Armed groups must consequently be separated from unarmed groups *stop* If the latter cannot resume their previous occupations they must disperse in small groups and await the time when we can arm them *stop* The armed groups must continue their guerrilla activities against enemy communications and harass them unremittingly stop.'

I had received a similar instruction before the Normandy landing. Though perfectly reasonable, it was hard to comply with on the ground. All the attendant risks notwithstanding, and in order to avoid demoralizing their men, most maquis commanders hung on to every one of their recruits.

Shortly afterwards London instructed me to be present at a designated landing site because an SOE officer wished to communicate with me by S-phone (walkie-talkie). It was an exciting and rewarding experience, if mainly from the aspect of morale, when I saw the aircraft circle at low altitude and, as I paced up and down the landing site, recognized Colonel Buckmaster's voice. Five minutes later the plane banked and headed back to England.

I welcomed the news that London had reassigned command of the Resistance because the unification of all combat units could only be beneficial — or so I thought.

In July I was informed that my immediate superior would henceforth be 'Ellipse', the regional military delegate. I had no objection to submitting to Ellipse's authority, though I never received any order or communication from him. We did meet towards the end of July and got on very well, but our encounter brought no change in the policy I had pursued since my arrival.

My relations with London were sometimes confused. I was informed that some commandos would land by parachute in the very near future, but the date of their arrival was repeatedly postponed. I was offered some highly qualified assistants, none of whom spoke good French, when all I wanted was arms, arms, and more arms. We were already well provided with the finest human material. At the end of June, however, London offered to send me an arms instructor who not only possessed excellent qualifications but was French as well. Jean-Pierre being overburdened with work, I accepted the offer, and my team of SOE *farfelus* acquired a fourth member. On the night of 1/2 July Lieutenant Marc Gerschel, code-name Gilbert, landed by parachute at Coursac, not far from Périgueux. Gilbert was an experienced *résistant*, not a greenhorn. Fearless and outgoing, he proved an excellent recruit.

Parachuting arms and equipment into occupied France entailed precise and meticulous organization. I have already referred to the careful assessments we undertook before deciding whether or not to supply a maquis group with arms. If our decision was favourable we had to find a site that would lend itself to an air drop. Generally speaking, the commander of the relevant group was able to suggest one. In such cases I would reconnoitre the site with Jean-Pierre or Paul Lachaud to see if it met our security requirements: if the arms could be swiftly evacuated, if German forces were far enough away, and if the lie of the land imposed no limitations.

Once we had agreed to recommend an air drop to London, we and the relevant maquis commander settled on a phrase which the BBC would broadcast on the night of the air drop itself, thus confirming that the operation was under way. Many maquis commanders liked to choose a phrase that held some personal significance. If not, my comrades or I would choose one at whim. There was nothing abstruse about the phrases we selected for the BBC. One of them, for example, was 'Jean-Pierre likes nuts'. This was simply because we had discovered that our friend Jean-Pierre (Peter Lake) had developed a passion for Périgord nuts.

Paul Lachaud, Jean-Pierre or I myself would then instruct the maquis commanders in the technique of preparing for an air drop. The site had to be marked out with beacons or headlights so that the pilot could identify it from the air, but the fires were not to be lit until we heard the sound of approaching engines. It was also essential, when the aircraft overflew the site, to use a torch to flash a code letter specified in advance by London. Unless this letter was recognized from the air, there was a danger that the pilot would fly off without dropping any containers.

The site had also to be approved by London. Its location was conveyed by means of an extremely simple system developed with the aid of Michelin maps. First we indicated the number of the map and the page. Then, by referring to a grid with letters and numerals along the horizontal and vertical axes respectively, we could pinpoint the spot. We also indicated the nearest village and its bearing in relation to our landing site. A typical message might read as follows: 'Suggest Map X, Page 8, Y28, Montfaucon 2 km.' Casimir would tap it out, adding our chosen phrase for the BBC. If London accepted our landing ground we received an indication of the approximate date of the air drop and the code letter to be used on site.

We duly instructed the maquis commander to prepare to receive an air drop within the said period, told him what code letter to use on site, and warned him to listen carefully for the BBC's message every night. For a long time I attended all the air drops. Thereafter I often delegated the job to Paul Lachaud or Jean-Pierre. From mid-July onwards, however, it was impossible for us to be present, and the maquisards, being well trained by then, managed without us.

The Air Drop at Moustoulat, 14 July, 1944

Although air drops in our area were becoming noticeably more frequent, we were once more short of the arms and equipment required for guerrilla warfare thanks to losses sustained in combat and, more particularly, to the growing numerical strength of the Resistance.

On 12 June, 1944, I had received the following message:

'No. 40 *stop*. In the event that we can carry out air drops in daylight, require to know the places where you may be able to organize this type of operation *stop* These operations cannot be carried out at low altitude, so may result in a wide dispersion of containers *stop* Can you confirm that your reception committees will be able to recover material? *stop* This type of operation will require recognition signals on the ground consisting of broad white and yellow strips at least three metres wide *stop* Messages referring to these operations will always be prefaced by the phrase "Important, for Nestor".'

This was news of considerable significance. We were sufficiently confident to confirm to London that we were capable of carrying out such operations, and I suggested some sites that struck me as suitable.

It was not until 30 June that things began to crystallize. The following message reached me:

'No. 53, re No. 40 of 12/6 *stop* Essential requirements for daylight air drop: first, landing site 3 by 3 km. minimum and perimeter under your complete control; secondly, your guarantee of sufficient personnel to receive and immediately dispose of material *stop* The consignment to be 400 containers minimum *stop* Scale of operation could lead to enemy intervention; thirdly, Casimir's presence on site indispensable until operation complete; fourthly, please guarantee no anti-aircraft fire within 15-mile radius *stop* If operation considered too hazardous unwilling risk it *stop* If not, will endeavour supply you from aircraft based North Africa.'

We had to act very quickly. Jean-Pierre, Poulou, Commandant Robert and I were agreed on two points. The first was that we could carry out such an operation, the second that the AS maquis of Vaujour and Guédin offered the best guarantees of success in respect of defence, security, and efficiency.

I passed the word to Malraux/Berger, who was most enthusiastic and decided to accompany us on our projected visit to Vaujour's maquis. I greatly respected the two regular army captains who had built up the AS maquis of Corrèze with such success, and had every confidence in them. Theirs was a well-disciplined, well-organized unit that had acquitted itself with great distinction in the course of numerous attacks on the enemy, notably when the 'Das Reich' division passed through our area. René Vaujour, alias Hervé, was officially in command because of his seniority in the army list, but Marius Guédin, alias Georges, was much more than a sidekick. Where the command structure and organization of this maquis was concerned, the two men divided their responsibilities extremely well. Vaujour had a brusque manner but proved an effective associate once the ice was broken. Guédin, less forthcoming to begin with, was an efficient and courageous officer. I got on well with both of them.

On reaching Vaujour's maquis we were surprised to encounter a third officer whom he introduced to us as Lieutenant-Colonel Jacquot. Taking me aside, Vaujour explained that the newcomer had just joined the unit, and that his arrival presented certain problems because Jacquot technically outranked both himself and Guédin. I was amused by this thoroughly military dilemma and asked Vaujour, ironically, if he intended to relinquish command of his unit to Jacquot. Vaujour smiled with narrowed eyes but said nothing.

Meanwhile, Jacquot had buttonholed Malraux and was eagerly plying him with an account of his previous career. He had, I think, been a member of Daladier's cabinet and knew a lot of people. Malraux seemed interested and mentioned a number of names familiar to Jacquot, or so he claimed. I decided to leave them to their conversation and informed Vaujour and Guédin of the reason for our visit. They were astonished to hear that the Allies were planning such a large-scale daylight air drop in our area, but they became very excited when I told them that, on reflection, I believed them to be the persons best qualified to help me carry out the operation successfully.

'The prime essential,' I said, 'is a large landing site that meets London's requirements.'

'That's not the problem,' Vaujour cut in. 'I've got the site you need, and I'll show it to you in due course. We're flattered that you should think of us, but the fact remains that you're inviting us to take part in a very risky operation. There's every chance the enemy will attack while the drop is in progress.'

'It's precisely because of that danger that I chose you, Hervé,' I replied.

Guédin, who had remained silent until then, suddenly snapped, 'These arms, who are they for?'

'Don't worry, Georges,' I told him. 'There'll be plenty for everyone. We'll be getting over four hundred containers, and your share will be a generous one. That's a promise.'

Guédin seemed satisfied.

'Let's go and inspect the site,' Vaujour suggested.

153

I set off by car with Vaujour, Guédin, Poulou and Jean-Pierre. The proposed landing site, a broad expanse of level ground, was not far away.

'Wonderful! We'll never find anywhere better.'

Poulou and Jean-Pierre went off to inspect the perimeter.

'Terrific!' was Jean-Pierre's verdict when he returned.

I explained my point of view on the way back.

'It's an immense responsibility, I know. The possibility of a fiasco can't be dismissed, as London fully accepts, and we can always turn the whole thing down. But if we stay on our toes, cordon off the landing site and get ready to evacuate the arms in double-quick time, I'm convinced that we'll succeed even if the Germans do attack, not that I think they will. If they don't know the planes have arrived until they're overhead, they'll be long gone and we'll have recovered the consignment by the time they get here from Brive. Anyway,' I concluded, 'we need those arms badly.'

'Jack,' said Vaujour, 'I honestly think we can pull it off after all.'

'It's insane,' said Guédin, 'but it's a must. We've got the resources to defend the site, and the outposts should be able to prevent the Boche from getting up there in time. We'll hold them off all right. This is a great moment for the Resistance.'

We were all very excited by now. Having thanked Vaujour and Guédin, I added a few administrative details.

'An air drop on this scale requires very careful preparation, so I'm going to leave Jean-Pierre with you. He'll represent me here for the next couple of weeks and organize the technical aspect of the drop on site. There'll be problems of communication, because London won't notify me until the very last moment that the operation is under way. I'll come at once, but you'll have to be in a permanent state of readiness five or six days from now.'

We rejoined Malraux and Jacquot in Vaujour's hut. They seemed to be getting on like a house on fire. Malraux, who had launched into one of his brilliant dissertations, was not in the least concerned when I told him of the agreement I had just reached. His thoughts were elsewhere.

Leaving Jean-Pierre with Vaujour and Guédin, I returned to La Poujade with Malraux and Poulou. Malraux seemed very happy – obviously, I thought, because the projected operation would undoubtedly be one of the most brilliant pieces of teamwork ever undertaken by the RAF and the Resistance. But no. Just as we reached the château, Malraux asked me what I thought of Jacquot.

'I hardly exchanged a word with him, André. I can't judge.'

'I see,' said Malraux. 'Well, I've just appointed him my second-in-command.'

And that was how Lieutenant-Colonel Jacquot, a newcomer to the Resistance, became 'Colonel Berger's' number two. He did, however, remain with the AS maquis of Corrèze and visited La Poujade on only one occasion.

I spent several days at La Poujade with Casimir, awaiting a message about our operation from London. London eventually approved the site, which was a preliminary triumph. Poulou at once left for Vaujour's maquis to inform him that the site had been accepted and assist Jean-Pierre in organizing the air drop.

Despite the importance of such an operation, it was impossible for me to remain closeted with the radio at La Poujade because I had some appointments in Corrèze and Dordogne that could not be postponed.

I should point out that cross-country trips were still hazardous at this period, and encounters with the Germans or the Milice were always on the cards. I used a car to get around, often accompanied by one or two bodyguards, and Dick the Alsatian seldom left my side. Travelling was dangerous and it was essential for me to remain in touch with La Poujade. This was not always easy. We could sometimes use the telephone, but this was risky and, in the case of visits to certain maquis units, impossible. We did, of course, have female couriers who would try to reach us if necessary, but we had to devise some solution to the problem of communication every time we moved.

I duly went off for two days, leaving Casimir at La Poujade. He was rather worried that London might transmit a signal about the Moustoulat operation in my absence, and he was right. On 10 July Casimir picked up an 'Important for Nestor' message. Although my itinerary was known at La Poujade, he panicked a little and asked London to get the BBC to contact me at once. Thanks to this piece of ingenuity I was surprised, while listening to the BBC, to hear 'Important message for Nestor – Return at once – Casimir.' I drove back the same night.

The message awaiting me at La Poujade read as follows:

'No. 4, 1300 hrs 10/7 *stop* Important for Nestor *stop* Large-scale daylight air drop scheduled 11 July onwards *stop* Ensure no anti-aircraft defences in vicinity *stop* Casimir to go to landing site *stop* Arrangements on ground three beacons in a triangle 200 metres apart, must be visible from 5 miles *stop* The fires to be lit in accordance with the following procedure *stop* The night before the operation the BBC will broadcast this message: "The red and green wheelbarrow belongs to . . ." *stop* The first letter of the name supplied will signify, according to its alphabetical position, the number of half-hours after 5 A.M. *stop* For example, the name "Désirée" indicates that the fires are to be lit at 7 A.M.'

There was no need to panic. We first had to receive the message 'Jean has had a good bath'. This would denote that the operation was under way, and that the air drop would take place within forty-eight hours. Casimir, who remained on listening watch during 11 and 12 July, exchanged several radio messages with London, who wanted to keep in regular touch in case our schedule had to be modified or postponed at the last minute. It was also stipulated that, once the BBC's message had been received, Casimir was to contact London every two hours in order to check on the progress of the operation.

At last, on the night of 12 July, the message came through. This meant that the drop was set for 14 July. Casimir remained in radio contact, and at dawn on 13 July I set off for Moustoulat with him and Madeleine, our courier.

It was imperative that Casimir communicate with London every two hours, but I could not be sure of completing the trip in that time. After driving for an hour and three-quarters, I estimated that it would take us at least another half-hour to reach Vaujour's maquis. Casimir was already fidgeting. I made an instant decision as we were driving through a village. Pulling up outside a house on the outskirts, I walked in, submachine-gun in hand, and lined the occupants up against a wall with their hands in the air. Madeleine remained on watch outside while Casimir followed me in with the suitcase containing his radio.

'Do you have a power point, please?' he inquired in his ultra-English accent.

He found a power point and started transmitting. The occupants of the house were very uneasy, but the paterfamilias had a sudden flash of enlightenment.

'*Mil.lediou!*' he exclaimed. 'You aren't Boches, you're English!' Losing all fear of my submachine-gun, he embraced us warmly. And, as so often happened in that hospitable part of the world, Casimir's transmission was followed by the opening of a good bottle of wine.

We finally reached Vaujour and Guédin, who inferred from my presence that the drop was imminent. Jean-Pierre and Poulou had done an excellent job preparing for it with the aid of the maquisards. Vaujour and Guédin themselves had concentrated on the defence of the landing site and its approaches. We spent most of the night checking details while Casimir frantically operated his Morse key.

The Moustoulat air drop took place at about 6 a.m. on 14 July, 1944. No less than four hundred and thirty-six containers were landed by parachute, enough to give all the maquis in the area a generous allocation of arms. What was more, we learned that George Hiller had carried out a similar operation at Loubressac in Lot. I know of very few whose eyes did not grow moist at the sight of such an impressive aerial armada traversing the skies over France at dawn on 14 July, 1944.

As General Lévy recounts in *Opération Cadillac: 14 juillet 1944* (Régirex, France, 1989), the Moustoulat air drop formed part of a huge, concerted operation organized by the Allies. It lent powerful support to the French Forces of the Interior in central and eastern France, the sectors in question being Vosges, Cantal, Corrèze, Ain, Dordogne, Lot, Haut-Vienne, Saône-et-Loire, and Creuse.

Operation Cadillac was genuinely successful. Of the 349 bombers that took part, escorted by 524 fighters, 320 attained their objectives. A total of 3791 containers, or 417 tonnes, of arms were dropped on the seven landing sites designated by the Supreme Command of the Allied Expeditionary Forces in Europe. (The Moustoulat air drop was officially code-named 'Digger'.)

General Gubbins, overall chief of the SOE, of which Colonel Buckmaster headed the French section, stated with some pride after the war that the air drop he mounted on 14 July, 1944, was the biggest ever carried out in an area extending from Norway to Indo-China and Burma.

Malraux turned up later that morning. He was very excited to see us hurriedly loading up the last of the arms containers and spiriting them away to safety, but he looked tired. He had re-established contact with my friend George Hiller and was starting to work as closely with him and the 'Veny' (Vincent) group as he did with me. I had been very busy in recent weeks, and our opportunities for a chat were fewer than before. He briefed me on his problems with certain maquis units, especially those belonging to the FTP.

'I'm worried,' he told me. 'They're playing a dangerous game. What will happen at the Liberation?'

He went on to talk of George Hiller, who was going to take him to see Colonel Vincent, commander of the Veny group.

'It could be constructive. I'm also hoping to visit Tarn.'

His misgivings about the FTP were well founded. I had lost touch with Vincent Bonnetot and my other FTP associates. They had been progressively replaced by men who were close to the Communist Party. The communists were putting out a certain amount of propaganda as the Liberation drew nearer, doubtless in the hope of gaining political control of the Resistance.

Malraux's remark foreshadowed his firm stand at the grand conference of the MLN [*Mouvement de Libération Nationale*] at the Mutualité, Paris, on 23 January, 1945.

After lunching with us and conferring awhile with Jacquot, Malraux set off for Lot.

I returned to La Poujade two days later. Casimir, whom I had so carefully hidden away for months, was exhilarated by his adventurous excursion to Moustoulat. He had made an important contribution to the success of the air drop. Jean-Pierre stayed on with Vaujour, who wanted to retain his services as a weapons instructor for a week or two.

Some days later Michel (Cyril Watney) turned up looking dog-tired and dejected. It was our first encounter since he had acted as my radio operator after Henri's arrest, and I knew, as soon as I set eyes on him, that his presence spelled trouble.

'Jack,' he said, 'I've got something to tell you. George Hiller has been badly wounded and Malraux is under arrest.'

Malraux's Arrest

George Hiller had accompanied Malraux to Tarn, as planned, and introduced him to the commander of the Veny group.

Malraux and George set off on the return journey accompanied by a senior member of the Veny group, Henri Collignon, a driver, Marius Loubare, and a bodyguard, Emilio Lopez. They took the road to Carjac and headed for Gramat along the D14, unaware that an enemy column had just entered Gramat and that the Germans had set up check-points on all the roads in the vicinity.

At about 5 p.m. George's car rounded a bend and found itself only a stone's throw from a road-block. The Germans opened fire at once, killing the driver instantly and bursting a tyre. The car ended upside down in a ditch. Collignon, George and Lopez managed to reach a small embankment, but George had been hit. With Lopez's assistance he succeeded in getting away despite his wound. Collignon went to ground in a copse. The Germans were too jumpy and unsure of themselves to pursue the *résistants,* and George, with a supreme effort, managed to put some distance between them and himself. He was bleeding profusely, so Lopez concealed him in a maize field, applied a makeshift tourniquet (a strip torn from his shirt), and went off to fetch help. He borrowed a bicycle and contrived to reach the maquis where Watney was.

Notwithstanding the efforts of Watney, Verlhac, and others, they failed to reach George until the next day, 23 July, by which time his condition was alarming. After a Dr Lachèze had treated him on the spot as best he could, George was taken to a small presbytery at Magnagues. There was no way of anaesthetizing him, so they made him drink three-quarters of a bottle of plum brandy to knock him out.

As soon as I heard the news from Watney I went off to see George, who was still in a desperate condition. Watney radioed a message to London, and the same night, 24 July, the SOE arranged an air drop of antigangrene and antitetanus serum. George turned the corner within hours, and London later sent an aircraft to pick him up and spirit him off to a hospital in England. He survived.

- CONVENTION DE REDDITION -

-:-:-:-:-:-:-:-:-:-:-:-:-:-:-

') - La ville de BRIVE étant encerclée depuis plusieurs jours par des forces
Françaises supérieures en nombre, le Colonel Commandant les troupes allemandes du département de la Corrèze déclare déposer les armes sans conditions,
en ce qui concerne la garnison de BRIVE, entre les mains des Forces Françaises de l'Intérieur, commandées par le Général KOENIG.- Il s'engage à facili-
ter la réddition des autres garnisons de Corrèze dépendant de lui.-

2°) - Les troupes allemandes seront traitées conformément aux lois de la guerre
telles qu'elles sont définies par les conventions internationales de LA HAYE,
les conventions de GENEVE et les déclarations des chefs des Gouvernements
Alliés sur les criminels de guerre.-

3°) - Une convention particulière interviendra immédiatement pour la garnison
de BRIVE.- D'autres conventions seront établies ultérieurement pour les autre
garnisons.- Elles éviteront toute vexations inutiles aux troupes allemandes.-
Jusqu'aux dates prévues par ces conventions particulières, les hostilités
seront poursuivies sans aucune réserve.-

4°) - Dès signature de la présente convention, les Français civils et militaires
incarcérés par les autorités allemandes seront libérés et dirigés sur l'Hôtel le plus important de la localité.- Les autorités allemandes répondent de
la sécurité de ces prisonniers jusqu'à l'arrivée des F.F.I.-

5°) - Le Lieutenant-Colonel F.F.I. JACQUOT et le Capitaine JACK de l'Armée Britan
nique sont chargés de la mise en application des conventions particulières.-
Ils en sont d'autre part solidairement garants.-

6°) - Tout le matériel de guerre ainsi que les approvisionnements seront livrés
intacts aux F.F.I.-

Aux avant-postes de Brive le 15 août 1944 à 21.3

TERMS OF SURRENDER

(1) The town of BRIVE having for several days been surrounded by numerically superior French forces, the colonel commanding the German troops in the Department of Corrèze states that, where the garrison of BRIVE is concerned, they will *unconditionally surrender their arms* to the French Forces of the Interior commanded by General KOENIG. He undertakes to facilitate the surrender of the other garrisons in Corrèze under his command.

(2) German troops will be treated in accordance with the rules of war as defined by the international conventions of THE HAGUE, the GENEVA conventions, and the declarations of the Allied heads of government in regard to war criminals.

(3) Surrender terms specific to the garrison of BRIVE will come into force with immediate effect. Other surrender terms will subsequently be laid down for the other garrisons. They will spare the German troops all unnecessary humiliation. Until the dates specified by these separate surrender terms, unrestricted hostilities will continue.

(4) Upon signature of the present terms, French civilians and military personnel imprisoned by the Germans will be released and taken to the largest hotel in the locality. The German authorities will be responsible for the safety of these prisoners until the arrival of the FFI.

(5) Lieutenant-Colonel JACQUOT of the FFI and Captain JACK of the British Army are charged with putting the separate terms into effect. They also jointly guarantee them.

(6) All war material and supplies will be turned over intact to the FFI.

On the outskirts of Brive, 2100, 15 August, 1944.
[THREE SIGNATURES AT FOOT]

Meanwhile, Malraux had been hit in the right leg just as he was laboriously extricating himself from the overturned car in the ditch. He lost consciousness and came round to find himself a prisoner.

Why hadn't the Germans shot him on the spot? We didn't know. He told me after his release that he had given his real name to the officer in command of the detachment, and that the latter, who happened to have heard of the writer André Malraux, had decided to take no action before consulting his superiors. Accordingly, Malraux was carted off to a prison in Toulouse.

The arrest of André Malraux/Colonel Berger caused consternation in Resistance circles and numerous schemes were devised to engineer his escape. Bernhardi and Rochebouet managed to get in touch with some people who claimed that they could bribe certain of the prison guards at Toulouse. I informed the authorities in London, who sent me the requisite money. Bernhardi and my father, Commandant Robert, went off to Toulouse with the cash. It was a very delicate and dangerous expedition and I sanctioned it only with the greatest reluctance. Bernhardi and Robert established contact with the relevant people and learned that other Resistance groups were generously participating in the operation. Although the sums disbursed to free Malraux probably assured him of more lenient treatment, no one succeeded in getting him out.

The memory of this operation has always rankled with me, because one way or another we were taken for a ride. André Malraux was eventually released from Saint-Michel Prison, Toulouse, when the Germans evacuated the city on 19 August, 1944.

As soon as I learned of Malraux's arrest I went to Vaujour's command post, accompanied by Jean-Pierre, to inform him of the sad news. I found Vaujour and Guédin with Lieutenant-Colonel Jacquot.

'Under these circumstances,' Jacquot calmly announced, 'it is my duty to assume command.'

The Liberation of Brive-la-Gaillarde

The air drop at Moustoulat on 14 July, 1944, had an unforeseen result. It played an indirect part in the negotiations that preceded the liberation of nearby Brive on 15 August, 1944 – Brive-la-Gaillarde, the first town in France to be liberated solely by the Resistance.

Some days after the Moustoulat air drop, Vaujour informed me that rumours were circulating in Brive about the aircraft that had overflown the town on 14 July. It was thought by some that they had landed a brigade of Allied commandos by parachute, and the German commander was inclined to believe this. At a meeting I attended with Vaujour, Guédin, Lieutenant-Colonel Jacquot and Jean-Pierre, we expressed our satisfaction with this version of events and urged that it be circulated as widely as possible, especially within the Germans' hearing.

Meanwhile, the maquisards were steadily tightening their grip on Brive and one or two skirmishes took place. The sub-prefect, Monsieur Chaussade, was not inactive. In the course of his meetings with the German C.O. he exaggerated the size of the maquis units in position around the town.

Jean-Pierre and I received some British uniforms by parachute. The situation became clearer during the second week of August and we learned by way of the sub-prefecture and some *résistants* who had remained in the town that the Germans wanted to parley. It was agreed that Commandants de Metz and Pierre, on behalf of the FFI, and Captain Peter Lake (Jean-Pierre no longer), on behalf of the Allies, would meet with a German plenipotentiary at Lanteuil. This first contact proved difficult. Our own representatives had been given clear instructions – 'the unconditional surrender of the German forces' – whereas the German plenipotentiary proved rather vague. Having requested that the Germans should retain their arms, relinquish only two-thirds of the town to the Resistance and remain in occupation of a predetermined sector, he left Lanteuil knowing that his proposal would never be accepted. We were all very worried that the situation might deteriorate with tragic results, especially as our men were raring for a fight.

— CONVENTION PARTICULIERE POUR LA REDDITION DE LA GARNISON DE BRIVE —

—:—:—:—:—:—:—:— :—:—:—:—:—:—:—:—:—

1°) La garnison de BRIVE déposera ses armes sans conditions le 15 Août à 23 H.

2°) — Les troupes allemandes tenant les barrages quitteront leurs positions à 22 H.
et rentreront au collège CABANIS.—

3°) — La garnison rassemblée au Collège CABANIS déposera ses armes et ses équipements
dans la cour d'Honneur du Collège et se rassemblera sur l'Avenue donnant accès
au Collège suivant les ordres du Capitaine VAUJOUR et du Capitaine GUÈDIN de la
Brigade A.S. de la Corrèze (F.F.I.).—

4°) — Les hostilités cesseront à 22 Heures.—

5°) — Le Lieutenant-Colonel F.F.I. JACQUOT, Interrégional F.F.I. et le Capitaine
JACK de l'Armée Britannique (Q.G. inté r lié) se portent solidairement garants
de la présente convention.—

6°) — Le Colonel Commandant la Garnison allemande se mettra à la disposition du
Lieutenant-Colonel F.F.I. JACQUOT et du Capitaine JACK pour établir les conventions de réddition éventuelles des autres garnisons de la Corrèze.—

7°) — Tout le matériel de guerre ainsi que les approvisionnements seront livrés
intacts aux F.F.I.

Aux Avant Postes de Brive le 15 Août 1944 à 21 H 15

F.F.I.
No. 5 District

TERMS OF SURRENDER SPECIFIC
TO THE GARRISON OF BRIVE

(1)   The garrison of BRIVE will lay down their arms unconditionally at 2300 on 15 August.

(2)   German troops manning road-blocks will quit their posts at 2200 and go to CABANIS College.

(3)   The garrison assembled at CABANIS College will deposit their arms and equipment in the school's central courtyard and assemble in the avenue leading to the school under the orders of Captain VAUJOUR and Captain GUÉDIN of the A.S. Brigade of Corrèze (F.F.I.).

(4)   Hostilities will cease at 2200.

(5)   Lieutenant-Colonel F.F.I. Jacquot of the Interregional F.F.I. and Captain JACK of the British Army (Inter-Allied H.Q.) jointly guarantee the present terms.

(6)   The colonel commanding the German garrison will make himself available to Lieutenant-Colonel F.F.I. Jacquot and Captain JACK to work out possible terms of surrender for the other garrisons in Corrèze.

(7)   All war material and supplies will be turned over intact to the F.F.I.

On the outskirts of Brive, 2115, 15 August, 1944.

[Five facsimile signatures]

On 15 August, 1944, we were informed that the German colonel wanted a meeting at the highest level, if possible that afternoon. Though wary of a trap, we agreed to meet with him. Lieutenant-Colonel Jacquot, Malraux's temporary replacement, was appointed to represent the FFI, and I acted as the representative of the Allies.

The meeting took place at Lanteuil, as before. After some preliminaries, Colonel Bohmer intimated that he was prepared to surrender but concerned for his men's safety thereafter. We emphasized that we were army officers, not irregulars, and that we would guarantee the prisoners' safety.

At 9.15 p.m. Bohmer signed the surrender document, which was countersigned on behalf of the Resistance by Lieutenant-Colonel Jacquot and me (I being the only one to use my *nom de guerre*. Vaujour and Guédin then joined us to draft the special terms relating to the surrender procedure. This document was countersigned on behalf of the Allies by Jacquot, Vaujour, Guédin, and myself.

An hour later we entered Brive, now liberated. The next day, not wanting him to learn of our little subterfuge concerning the Allied paratroops from anyone else, I paid a call on Colonel Bohmer. He took the news in good part.

'*C'est de bonne guerre,*' he observed, but he was far more taken aback to learn that I was the Captain Jack whom the Gestapo had been hunting for so long.

Discounting the maquisards' bravery and the sub-prefect's powers of persuasion, I think that the surrender of Brive owed much to Colonel Bohmer's realization of the predicament of the German armies in Europe and the size of the maquis forces surrounding Brive, not to mention the possible presence of a highly-trained brigade of paratroops.

The entry of Resistance forces into Brive was a memorable event and one that triggered a positive explosion of joy. The streets were lined with cheering townsfolk, almost every one of whom had turned out for the occasion.

I myself entered Brive accompanied by Jean-Pierre and Casimir. Standing in the back of our open car, we saluted the crowd with an ultra-martial air, like captains of war. Deep down, though, we were as moved as everyone else.

While we were slowly approaching the centre of the town,

I suddenly caught sight of a young man applauding us in the crowd. His face looked familiar. I jumped off the moving car and, to the great surprise of the onlookers, grabbed him by the collar. It was Minangois, the young militiaman who had almost got me arrested at Martel with Maurice Arnouilh.

I must make it clear that my account of the liberation of Brive has been confined to such incidents as I witnessed at first hand. Other people merit recognition as well, because the maquisards on the periphery of Brive and the *résistants* within its walls played a vital part in liberating the town.

Exeunt the British!

The Germans were starting to evacuate the whole of the south-west. News of Malraux's release reached us on 19 August, 1944. We looked forward to seeing him again, but he kept us waiting awhile before he finally turned up at La Poujade.

He was in a state of high excitement. Now that almost the whole of our area had been liberated, he had other plans in mind. With infectious enthusiasm, he announced that he had decided to form a brigade of Alsatians and Lorrainers in the south-west and set off to liberate Strasbourg.

'Jack,' he said, 'you've got to help me. Do you still have some arms stashed away?'

I did my best for him, and he set off with his splendid Alsace-Lorraine Brigade, of which Lieutenant-Colonel Jacquot assumed command. Before he left I revealed my true nationality. I never discovered whether or not he resented my having concealed it from him for so long.

Commandant Robert left to visit a maquis over towards Bergerac and returned with my Uncle Marcel. That was when I learned that another member of my family belonged to a maquis unit in the area. I decided that the time had come to tell everyone that I was French and that Robert was my father. Quite a few jaws dropped at this revelation!

Learning that the Germans were holding out on the Île d'Oléron, I made a trip to Marennes in the belief that it might be interesting to organize a Resistance network on the island from the mainland – a kind of SOE in miniature. I assigned

Jean-Pierre and, later, Gilbert to try something along those lines, and 'Operation Bickford' was born.

'*Résistants nouveaux*' – 'the moth-balled ones', as we derisively called them – were surfacing everywhere. I sensed that our mission was drawing to a close. Peter Lake was invited by some friends at Marennes to join them in welcoming General de Gaulle when he passed through Saintes. Peter was very proud and moved to see de Gaulle. One of the 'mothballed ones' must have bad-mouthed him in advance, however, because he got a frigid reception when introduced. De Gaulle stared at him.

'Your name?'

'Jean-Pierre, *mon général*.'

'That's not a name.'

'It's my *nom de guerre, mon général*.'

'You're English. You've no business here, go away!' And the general turned his back on him.

Peter was shattered. Fortunately, his friends rallied round and consoled him. What would Malraux have said, had he been there – and what, for heaven's sake, would I!

Captain Peter Lake, holder of the *Légion d'honneur* and the Military Cross, was very hurt by this incident. Some years later, however, when he was the British Consul in Brazil, our ambassador specially invited him to an all-French reception at Rio de Janeiro in honour of General de Gaulle, who was there on an official visit. This time de Gaulle greeted him in a charming manner, and Peter was tactful enough not to remind him of the incident at Saintes.

'I've made my peace with your general,' Peter told me on the telephone some days after this second encounter.

My feelings for de Gaulle have never changed despite his insult to my British comrade-in-arms, if only for this one reason: he salvaged the honour of France, and we were not, thanks to him, on the losing side when the war ended.

What would our fate have been if Pétain's collaboration in the name of the French people were the only memory that lingered on, together with that of some seven hundred thousand Frenchmen conscripted for work in Germany and some sixty-six thousand Jews deported under the auspices of the Vichy régime?

Our penultimate message from London came through on 15 September, 1944. It announced that our mission was at an end and informed us that a plane would be coming to pick us up at Le Blanc in Indre and fly us back to England. We were also told that our radio link would be severed with effect from 16 September, and that from now on we must communicate through the regional military delegate. Not knowing where to find the DMR, we were in something of a quandary. With a final effort, Casimir managed to obtain the date of our departure from Le Blanc. This last message further informed me that I had just been promoted major.

We had only a few days in which to wind things up, so I entrusted the liquidation of our network to my father. I said goodbye to all my friends, kissed our wonderful Marguerite Brouillet and our beloved Georgette, and the four of us *farfelus* set off for Le Blanc, but not without spending a memorable night at Limoges and receiving a liquid welcome at Cognac on the way.

The plane was waiting for us at the airport, but we had some difficulty in finding our pilots. They were being fêted by the vast majority of the local inhabitants, theirs being the first Allied aircraft to land in the area since the Liberation. In high spirits, the crew shepherded us aboard.

It was *au revoir* to France once more. We were quiet during the flight until Peter Lake suddenly spotted that we were about to cross the English coast near his home and told the pilot. The latter, just to be friendly, flew us along the village street at treetop height, but we landed in London safe and sound. It was over.

The next day, five officers in spanking new uniforms congregated at Claridge's, where they took a table and ordered some soup and wine. When the head waiter brought it, Major Jacques Poirier and Captains Watney, Lake, Beauclerk and Gerschel rose, came to attention, and toasted each other in what was probably the first and only *chabrol** ever consumed at a leading London hotel.

---

*See footnote on p.100

EPILOGUE

Allied forces were meeting less and less resistance, and it was rumoured that Germany would soon surrender. I had been back in Paris for several weeks, waiting to be reassigned. I was French once more. I wore the uniform of a paratroop major, but I had been attached to the DGER*, and it seemed ever clearer to me that I was being made to pay for having joined the British SOE.

I often visited the Paris branch of the SOE. Although I met sundry friends there, my main purpose was to obtain news of Henri Peulevé, Charles Delsanti, Roland Malraux and Louis Bertheau. Where the last three were concerned, the news was bad. It seemed certain that Delsanti and Roland Malraux had died at Lübeck. This hypothesis was confirmed. During the heavy bombardment that immediately preceded the Allies' capture of the port, the Nazis had seen fit to chain concentration camp survivors together and put them aboard the most exposed ships in the harbour, where they could serve as a buffer between Allied and German troops. We also learned that Louis Bertheau had died in Sandbostel concentration camp.

Malraux came to Paris and invited me to dine with him. It was a surprising evening. I had imagined that we would

*Direction Générale d'Études et de Renseignements, successor to the London-based BCRA [Bureau Central de Renseignement et d'Action] (see footnote on p.87).

171

have a quiet dinner at some good restaurant, but Malraux announced that we were both the guests of General Corniglion Molinier, whom I had never met.

It was a glittering reception, and we were warmly welcomed, but I very soon gathered that the real object of the evening was a meeting between Malraux and Sir Alexander Korda, who was on his way through Paris. Malraux, who was in fine form, enthused to me after dinner about the Alsace-Lorraine Brigade. Before we went our separate ways he confided that he would have an interesting proposition for me in the very near future. Some days later he was appointed a minister in General de Gaulle's cabinet and offered me a post as French Ambassador to Canada.

While visiting SOE headquarters in London I was asked by Vera Atkins to go and see Bourne Patterson. When I walked into his office, accompanied by Vera, he shook me warmly by the hand. Then, to my astonishment, he announced that His Majesty King George VI was going to invest me with the Distinguished Service Order, and that I would soon have to return to London to receive it from his hands at Buckingham Palace.

'That's great news,' I said.

'Here's another bit of good news,' Vera broke in. 'Henri will be in Paris in three days' time.'

My reunion with Henri was a memorable occasion. We had so much to tell each other that we hardly stopped to draw breath. Eventually we decided to celebrate our reunion by dining at the Tour d'Argent, no less. Though still very weak after his recent ordeal, Henri was in sparkling form and did full justice to the superb meal.

At the next table two couples were conversing in loud voices, notably a podgy little man who roared with laughter at the least excuse. I could hear snatches of what he was saying to his neighbour.

'Take my son, for example . . . While the other youngsters were traipsing off into the countryside and playing at soldiers with the Fifi [presumably, the FFI], he was studying hard. He'll be graduating from the Polytechnique this year!' That subject exhausted, he turned to another. 'Just imagine,' he blurted out, 'they've had the gall to arrest Castellane! I mean, how could he possibly have declined to co-operate with the Germans? Take my own case, for instance . . .' Then, realizing that we could hear him, he lowered his voice.

'I've half a mind to punch him on the jaw,' I said.

I looked at Henri. He was happy. He pored over the bill, produced some notes from his pocket, and paid. Then, with a broad smile, he got up to leave.

'You see, Jack, it's over. That was the last meal we'll ever have on the SOE. From now on we'll have to earn our own living, the two of us.'

FORTY YEARS AFTER

I've been drifting off Théoule for a good hour. I'm at least eight miles out and alone on board, but dolphins are making a fuss of me all round the boat. Seated in the bow with my legs dangling over the side, I marvel at their agility.

I day-dream awhile, and my thoughts go back to the time that left such a mark on us – over forty years ago now! I think first of the companions who have left us, one by one, since the end of the war. My father, Colonel Robert Poirier of the French Air Force, killed in a crash in 1949; my old friend Charles the Bolshevik, back in 1946; my comrade-in-arms Henri Peulevé, who died one night at Madrid in the 1960s; George Hiller, a brilliant diplomat, at Brussels in 1962, after a long and painful illness; Maurice Arnouilh; Paul 'Poulou' Lachaud; Alain Born, friend of my youth; René Boilet, alias Gisèle; Deschamps; Yves Peron, alias Caillou; René Vaujour, alias Hervé, commander of the AS maquis in Corrèze; General Jacquot; the Verlhacs; Abbé Marchadoux, parish priest of Sagelat, who baptized my son Richard; my dear friend Georges (later General) Guédin of the maquis of Corrèze; and many others. De Gaulle, Malraux – the list is a long one and grows longer every day. One more reason, perhaps, for writing this book!

But there are still a few of us left. Peter Lake, alias Jean-Pierre, did well in the British consular service – his postings included Paris, Iceland, Rio, and Venice – and has now settled down in Cambridge with his wife Kay. I was a witness at their wedding years ago, and our reunions are always a delight. Ralph Beauclerk, alias Casimir, became a successful banker but now lives quietly near London. I met him by chance in Saigon during a trip to the Far East in 1967. As modest and retiring as ever, Ralph seldom sends me news of himself. I miss his company. I sometimes see Marc Gerschel, who divides his time between Paris and Dordogne. Cyril Watney lives in England. Vera Atkins comes to stay with us every year. Of my friends in Dordogne and Corrèze, the following survive: Georgette, now Madame Robert, Nandoue Vidalie, Madeleine Bleygeat, Christian Plaçais, Lucien Gambelon, alias Michel. Dear Marguerite Brouillet left us recently, but I still see her daughter Monette, of whom I am very fond. My mother, 'Kiou', was still alive when I started to write this book but has since departed – alas! – in her ninety-fifth year.

As for me, I joined a large oil company after the war and held numerous jobs, first in Africa, then in South America (Venezuela and Argentina), and finally Europe (England, the Netherlands, France). Now I'm retired.

The dolphins are still circling the boat . . .

Many books continue to be published about the war years and the Resistance. They often refer to Pétain, who seems to be coming back into vogue. An old man who collaborated with the enemy, scattered millions of his compatriots to the four winds, encouraged them to serve Hitler, and sent 76,000 Jews to their deaths in concentration camps and 650,000 French workers to contribute to the Nazi war effort, he succeeded in performing that feat simply because he was a Marshal of France.

It appears, moreover, that freedom of thought must be the principle that governs everything written on this subject. The collaborators are now extolled for their talent and intelligence, even for their genius. Personally, I thought it was those very qualities that should have dissuaded them from betraying their country. Are we really expected to mourn Robert Brasillach, the author and Nazi sympathizer executed for treason in 1945, who advocated that Paul Reynaud and Georges Mandel be strung up and the French community purged of Jews?

It is true, after all, that certain French politicians claiming to be the heirs of General de Gaulle sometimes contemplate electoral pacts with those who regard the gas chambers as a mere bagatelle.

And I always thought de Gaulle had been the first to summon us not to bend the knee to Nazism! When asked who he was on television the other night, some French teenagers had no idea!

France is eternal; she will survive all these things. Like de Gaulle, I have always cherished 'a certain idea' of her.

The dolphins have swum off . . .

March 1990

APPENDICES

AIR DROP MESSAGES

Major Jacques Poirier's NESTOR/DIGGER network organized over eighty air drops during his mission in France. Listed below are a few of the warning orders transmitted by the BBC (some of them complete with map references):

Le Général a trois étoiles
[The General has three stars]
      (Michelin 75, p. 9. V29, Tulle 8 km. S)

Le coq est anémique
[The cockerel is anaemic]
      (Michelin 75, p. 5, G15, Bourdeilles 1 km. W)

Les farfelus sont réunis
[The madcaps are reunited]
      (Michelin 75, p. 9, Y22, Beynat 7 km. SE)

J'ai pris un bon bain
[I've had a good bath]
Mon réticule est vide
[My string bag is empty]
      (Michelin 75, p. 9, V18, Beynat 1.5 km. SE)

Les acacias sont des roses de Marie
[The acacias are Marie's roses]
>   (Michelin 75, p. 2, V26, Saussac 6 km. SE)

Évitez les marais fangeux
[Avoid the boggy marshes]
Fernande est amoureuse
[Fernande is in love]
>   (Michelin 72, p. 20, S29, Gentious 9 km. SE)

Le chien de Robert
[Robert's dog]
Le crocodile a la pépie
[The crocodile is parched]
>   (Michelin 75, p. 5, X21, Couloumieux 8 km. S)

Gribouille porte un monocle
[Tomfool is wearing a monocle]
Sophie s'est rasé les sourcils
[Sophie has shaved off her eyebrows]
Le crapaud vole
[The toad is flying]
>   (Michelin, 75, p. 5, p. 26, Couloumieux 15 km. SW)

Le rendez-vous est dimanche prochain
[The rendezvous is next Sunday]
Les cerises sont bonnes cette année
[The cherries are good this year]
Mon chien a mangé le foie qras
[My dog has eaten the foie gras]
>   (Michelin 75, p. 6, S19, Thenon 7 km. SW)

Jean-Pierre aime les noix
[Jean-Pierre likes nuts]
Liou est très gentille
[Kiou is very sweet]
>   (Michelin 75, p. 1, S24, Campagnac 1 km. SE)

On reconstruit la maison de Georgette
[Georgette's house is being rebuilt]
(Michelin 80, p. 1, V17, Rignac 2 km. S.)

Lucien n'ira plus au Puy-de-Dôme
[Lucien won't go to Puy-de-Dôme any more]
Le terrain est en friche
[The land is fallow]
Nous l'attendons impatiemment
[We're eagerly awaiting it]
(Michelin 75, p. 16, 012, Belves 6 km. NW)

Jean est un bon garçon
[Jean is a good fellow]
Charles est de bon humeur
[Charles is in a good mood]
(Boris. Michelin 75, p. 16, Q29, Saint-Cyprien 8 km. SW)

J'aime le foie gras
[I like foie gras]
(Michelin 75, p. 4, V21, Saint-Astier 7 km. SW)

Robert a bien soigné Dick
[Robert has taken good care of Dick]
(Michelin 75, p. 4, N21, Mussidan 6 km. NNE)

Le temps du mépris tire à sa fin
[The time for contempt is drawing to a close]
Flora a le cou rouge
[Flora's neck is red]
(Michelin 75, p. 6, Thenon 2 km. S)

Nous boirons bientôt le kirsch d'Alsace
[We'll soon be drinking Alsatian kirsch]
(Michelin 75, p. 15, U14, Saint-Alvère 3 km. NE)

Le moustique danse
[The mosquito is dancing]
(Michelin 75, p.5, 125, Couloumieux 17 km. SW)

L'autruche se tape le ventre
[The ostrich is patting its stomach]
On a récupéré Vincent
[Vincent has been retrieved]
                    (Michelin 75, p. 17, V14, Marcillac 2 km. E)

Georges est tombé par terre
[George has fallen to earth]
                    (Bertrand Michelin 75, p. 4, V28, Riberac 5 km. SW)

Après quatre jours sans sommeil
[After four sleepless days]
                    (Michelin 79, p. 6, W11, Biron 1 km. SW)

Garde à vous Turenne
[Come to attention Turenne]
                    (Michelin 75, p. 5, R19, Coursac 3 km. W)

J'espère qu'elle est jolie
[I hope she's pretty]
                    (Michelin 75, p. 8, P18, Douzenac 7 km. NW)

Aux audacieux les mains pleines
[Full hands to the bold]
                    Michelin 75, p. 4, X21, Mussidan 6 km. NW)

Antoine et Jacques sont deux copains
[Antoine and Jacques are a couple of pals]
                    (Michelin 75, p. 9, M25, Gramat 13 km. SW)

Nous Pensons à Raymond
[We're thinking of Raymond]
La crème est bonne chez le docteur
[The cream at the doctor's is good]
                    (Michelin 75, p. 7, p. 12, Juillac 3 km. N.)

ORGANIZATIONS REFERRED TO BY THEIR INITIALS

AS	Armée Secrète
BCRA	Bureau Central de Renseignement et d'Action
CNR	Conseil National de la Résistance
DMR	Délégué Militaire Régional
FFI	Forces Françaises de l'Intérieur
FTP	Francs-Tireurs et Partisans
MLN	Mouvement de Libération Nationale
MOI	Mouvement Ouvrier International
MUR	Mouvement Uni de la Résistance
OSS	Office of Strategic Services
SOE	Special Operations Executive
STO	Service du Travail Obligatoire

INDEX OF PERSONAL
AND CODE NAMES

VI-VII	BELLEDIN, Escot, member of the 'Nestor'/ 'Digger' network.(†)
VI-VII	BELLEDIN, Flora, courier of the 'Nestor'/ 'Digger' network.(†)
VI-VII	BERGER or COLONEL BERGER, see MAL-RAUX, André.
VI-VII	BERGERET, code name of Maurice LOUPIAS, commander of the Bergerac maquis and prefect of Bergerac.(†)
VI-VII	BERNHARDI, Pierre, member of the 'Nestor'/ 'Digger' network.
V-VII	BERTHEAU, Louis, radio operator of the 'Author' network, arrested and deported to Germany, where he died.(†)
VII	BOHMER, Colonel Heinrich, commander of the German garrison of Brive-la-Gaillarde.(†)
VI-VII	BOILET, René, alias GISÈLE, commander of the AS in Dordogne.(†)
V-VI	BONNETOT, Vincent, known as VINCENT, departmental chief of the FTP.(†)
I-II	BORN, Alain, friend of Jacques POIRIER at Cannes.(†)
	BOUDER, Serge, member of the "Jack" network in south-east France. Arrested by the Germans, he jumped from a moving train while en route for a concentration camp.
IV	BOURNE-PATTERSON, Major, member of French Section at SOE Headquarters, London.
VI-VII	BROUILLET, Marguerite, wife of Robert BROUILLET, an indefatigable member of the Resistance.(†)

VI-VII	BROUILLET, Robert, alias CHARLES 'the Bolshevik', member of the 'Nestor'/ 'Digger' network.(†)
IV-VII	BUCKMASTER, Colonel Maurice, head of the SOE's French Section, London.

C

CAILLOUX, see PÉRON.

VI	CAMUS, Albert, French writer.(†)
VI-VII	CARLOS, code name of Henri ORDEIG, commander of the MOI maquis.

CASIMIR, see BEAUCLERK.

CHARLES 'the Bolshevik', see BROUILLET, Robert.

VI-VII	CHATEAURENAUD, Émile, member of the 'Nestor'/'Digger' network, killed in action.(†)
VII	COMMARQUE, Gérard, Marquis de, résistant, owner of the Château de la Poujade, shot by the Germans.(†)
VI-VII	COUSTELLIER, René, alias SOLEIL, commander of the 'Soleil' group.

D

VI-VII	DELSANTI, Charles, member of the 'Author' network, arrested and died in Germany.(†)

DESCHELETTE, Eugène, see ELLIPSE.

DIGGER, SOE network, see Jacques POIRIER.

E

ELLIPSE, code name of DESCHELETTE, Eugène, Regional Military Delegate.

ESCOT, see BELLEDIN, Escot.

F

FLORA, see BELLEDIN, Flora.

G

VI-VII GAMBELON, Lucien, alias MICHEL, member of the 'Soleil' group, later of the 'Nestor'/ 'Digger' network.

VI-VII GAUCHER, André, alias MARTIAL, commander of the regional AS.

GEORGES, see GUÉDIN.

GERSCHEL, Marc, alias GILBERT, SOE officer landed by parachute to join 'Nestor'/ 'Digger' network.

VI GIDE, André, French writer.(†)

GILBERT, see GERSCHEL.

GISÈLE, see BOILET.

VI-VII GUÉDIN, Marius, later General, alias GEORGES, AS commander in Corrèze.(†)

VII GUNZBOURG, Philippe, Baron de, alias PHILI-BERT, leading member of HILAIRE's SOE network.(†)

187

H

HERVÉ, see VAUJOUR.

HILAIRE, see STARR.

III–IV–V– HILLER, George, alias MAXIME, head of the
VI–VII   'Footman' network.(†)

J

JACK or JACK L'ANGLAIS, see POIRIER, Jacques.

JEAN, see PEULEVÉ.

JEAN-PIERRE, see LAKE.

VII   JACQUOT, Pierre-Élie, later General, MALRAUX's
second-in-command and commander of the Alsace-
Lorraine Brigade.(†)

K

I–V   KIOU, pet name of Mme POIRIER, wife of Robert
and mother of Jacques.(†)

L

V–VI   LACHAUD, Georgette, now Mme Robert, leading
member of the 'Nestor'/'Digger' network.

V–VI–VII   LACHAUD, Paul, alias POULOU, field organizer of
air drops for the 'Nestor'/ 'Digger' network.(†)

VI–VII   LAKE, Peter, alias BASIL or JEAN-PIERRE, SOE
officer parachuted in to join the 'Nestor'/ 'Digger'
network.

V   LE HARIVEL, Jean, alias PHILIPPE, SOE officer
parachuted into France in 1941. We owe him the

excellent account (on pp.67–9) of the first air drop of men and equipment into France.

VI   LESCURE, Jean, author and *résistant*. Prominently engaged in producing clandestine publications under the occupation, he put JACK up during the latter's visit to Paris.

LOUPIAS, Maurice, see BERGERET.

M

VI-VII   MADELEINE, full name Madeleine BLEYGEAT, courier of the 'Nestor'/'Digger' network.

V-VI-VII   MALRAUX, André, alias Colonel BERGER, FFI chief and associate of the 'Nestor'/ 'Digger' network, commander of the Alsace-Lorraine Brigade, author and cabinet minister.(†)

V-VII   MALRAUX, Roland, brother of André, member of the SOE's 'Author' network, arrested and deported to Germany, where he died.(†)

VI   MARCHADOUX, Abbé, parish priest of Sagelat, Dordogne, and later of Siorac, Périgord.(†)

V-VI   MARÉCHAL, Raymond, commander of the 'Author' network's irregulars, arrested and gunned down by the Germans.(†)

MARTIAL, see GAUCHER.

MARTINS, the, family friends of the POIRIERS, Bordeaux-Arcachon.

MAURICE, see ARNOUILH or NUSENBAUM.

MAXIME, see HILLER.

MICHEL, see GAMBELON or WATNEY.

II   MISSON, neighbour of the POIRIERS at Mougins, introduced Jacques to the Resistance.

N

NANDOUE, see VIDALIE.

NESTOR, see POIRIER, Jacques.

VI-VII   NUSENBAUM, Maurice, SOLEIL's second-in command.

P

IV   PARK, factotum of the SOE's French Section in London.

VI   PAULHAN, Jean, French essayist and literary critic.(†)

III   PÉCHERAL, Jacques, journalist. Interned at Jaraba, he escaped with Henri PEULEVÉ.

V–
Epilogue   PÉRON, Yves, alias CAILLOUX, FTP commander in Dordogne, Deputy.(†)

PETERS, see POIRIER, Jacques.
PEULEVÉ, Henri, Henry, or Harry, alias JEAN, head of the SOE's 'Author' network, arrested and deported to Germany.(†)

II-III
IV-V
Epilogue

PHILIBERT, see GUNZBOURG, de.

VI-VII   PLAÇAIS, Christian, member of the 'Nestor' /'Digger' network.

I-VII   POIRIER, Robert, alias COMMANDANT ROBERT, father of Jacques, member of the 'Nestor'/ 'Digger' network, colonel in the French Air Force.(†)

I   POIRIER, Raymond, brother of Jacques.(†)

V

VI-VII   VAUJOUR, René, alias HERVÉ, commander of AS maquis in Corrèze.(†)

V   VERLHAC, Jean and Marie, members of George HILLER's 'Footman' network.(†)

VI   VIDALIE, Fernande, nicknamed NANDOUE, member of the 'Nestor'/'Digger' network.

VINCENT, see BONNETOT.

W

IV-V
VI-VII   WATNEY, Cyril, alias MICHEL, SOE radio operator parachuted in to join the 'Footman' network, assumed command thereof after George HILLER was wounded and evacuated.

IV   WATNEY, Walter, uncle of Cyril, owner of the Delage automobile company.(†)

IV-V   WILKINSON, George, SOE officer, deported to Germany, where he died.(†)

Y

YEO-THOMAS, Wing-Commander F.F.E., British agent (RF Section), escaped from Buchenwald with Harry PEULEVÉ, author of the book "The White Rabbit".